The Essex House Masque

Medieval & Renaissance Literary Studies

The
Essex House Masque of 1621

Viscount Doncaster
and the Jacobean Masque

Timothy Raylor

DUQUESNE UNIVERSITY PRESS
Pittsburgh, Pennsylvania

Published in the United States of America by:

DUQUESNE UNIVERSITY PRESS
600 Forbes Avenue
Pittsburgh, Pennsylvania 15282

Library of Congress Cataloging-in-Publication Data

Raylor, Timothy
    The Essex House masque of 1621: Viscount Doncaster and the Jacobean masque / Timothy Raylor.
        p.   cm. —(Medieval & Renaissance literary studies)
    Includes text of the Essex House masque.
    Includes bibliographical references and index.
    ISBN 0–8207–0310–9
    1. Essex House masque.   2. Carlisle, James Hay, Earl of, 1580–1636—Art and patronage.   3. Authors and patrons—England—History—17th century.   4. English drama—17th century—History and criticism.   5. Masques—History and criticism.   6. Metamorphosis in literature.   7. Giants in literature.   I. Essex House masque.   II. Title.   III. Series.
    PR2411.E75 R38 1999 2000
        822'.05—dc21   99–6669
                                                                              CIP

Printed on acid-free paper.

To the memory
of
Jeremy Maule
(1952–1998)

Contents

Illustrations

PREFACE

Recent years have seen an extraordinary expansion in our understanding of the Stuart court masque: the work of D. J. Gordon, Stephen Orgel, Graham Parry, Leah Marcus, David Lindley, Martin Butler, and James Knowles has reshaped our understanding of the form and its history. There remain, however, many gaps in our knowledge. A number of texts survive for masques whose occasion and authorship are obscure, and still more masques are known to have taken place for which no texts are extant. One of the most significant gaps in this respect was, until recently, what we might call the 'lost' festive season of 1620–21. While it may not have been as vigorous and varied as that of the previous year, it was by no means subdued: in addition to tilting, running at the ring, and a masque presented by the Middle Temple, two masques were performed at court. One of these was presented by Prince Charles at Whitehall on Twelfth Night (6 January 1621) before the two French ambassadors then in London; it was repeated at Shrovetide for the Spanish ambassador. While the royal budget in this time of fiscal crisis may only have stretched to a single masque, a second was offered to the king, the court, and the visiting French ambassador extraordinary on 8 January by James Hay, Viscount Doncaster, at Essex House. It was until recently assumed that the texts of both these masques had been lost. In 1992, however, Martin Butler demonstrated that the prince's masque of 1621 was, in fact, the well-known *Pan's Anniversary*—a masque traditionally assumed to have been performed during the previous summer. Butler's announcement marked a major step towards a reconstruction of the lost season. That reconstruction may now be completed, for a manuscript text came to light among the Portland Papers at the University of Nottingham in the summer of 1995 that can be identified as a copy of the libretto for the masque performed at Essex House.

The discovery of that text and its identification as the *Essex House Masque* were announced in *English Manuscript Studies 1100–1700* 7 (1998): 86–130. There I undertook a codicological and paleographical examination of the manuscript, and sought to present a semi-diplomatic edition of the masque text. That examination and text underlie the work presented here, and I am grateful to Dr. Peter Beal, the journal's editor, and to the British Library, its publisher, for permission to draw on that discussion. A preliminary investigation into the design and authorship of the masque was offered in *Medieval & Renaissance Drama in England* 10 (1998): 218–37. I am grateful to Dr. John Pitcher, editor of the journal, and to the Associated University Presses, its publisher, for allowing me to draw on that investigation here. This book does not reprint either of these articles; rather, it builds on the groundwork there laid to provide the first full study of the masque in its cultural and political contexts.

The book is divided into two parts. The first presents a lightly edited, un-modernized text supplemented by a commentary providing glosses and pointing to classical sources and contemporary parallels. In the second part of the book, the occasion and diplomatic function of the masque are examined; its structure, sources, and staging are analyzed; and the question of who invented, designed, and wrote it is investigated: Inigo Jones and George Chapman are proposed as collaborators.

As a record of an important diplomatic entertainment, an event that took place at a decisive moment in the crisis that precipitated Europe into the chaos of the Thirty Years War, the new text has an obvious historical significance. It is also a valuable addition to the surviving corpus of masques. In its assured and innovative use of conventional material, its dramatic and intellectual coherence, and its establishment of resonant relationships between the performers and their roles, *The Essex House Masque* can reasonably be seen as the finest of Lord Doncaster's masques, and as one of the most elegant, spectacular, and unified masques of the entire Stuart period.

An understanding of the masque helps us to make better sense of the masquing climate of the early 1620s, affording a fresh perspective on the background to Jonson's *Gypsies Metamorphosed*, in particular. In its promotion of views other than those of the king himself, it provides new evidence for the flexibility of the masque form. Most importantly, perhaps, the continuities now revealed between the several masques in which Doncaster was centrally involved (including *Lord Hay's Masque* and *Lovers Made Men*) invite us to look seriously at Doncaster's significance as a sponsor of the masque.

Because he cultivated no faction, Doncaster's political significance is easily overlooked; yet he remained, for the whole of James's reign and the first decade of Charles's, at the very heart of the court, exerting influence in both foreign and domestic affairs. Without a faction, the masque was one of the major channels for the expression of his goals. Not only was he one of its most liberal private patrons—exceeding, perhaps, even George Villiers, duke of Buckingham—he was also one of the most innovative and discerning. The distinctive character of *The Essex House Masque*, with its metamorphic action, involving the transformation of antimasquers into masquers, and its obsession with the power and lawful conduct of love, helps us to recognize a series of distinctively Doncastrian productions, continental in character and innovative in form, running through the *Lord Hay's Masque* and *Lovers Made Men*—a line that points the way towards the French fashions of the following reign. The delineation of this series helps us to acknowledge Doncaster as a vital link between the French *ballet* and the English masque prior to the arrival of the French queen, and allows us to detect his influence behind the sudden fashion for masques turning on metamorphoses in the period 1619–21.

The research underlying this monograph was made possible by the financial support of Carleton College and that of the Folger Shakespeare Library, where, in the early part of 1996, I held a Folger/National Endowment for the Humanities Short-Term Fellowship. In the course of my work I have studied in the Folger, the Hallward Library of Nottingham University, the Houghton Library at Harvard University, the British Library (where Mr. Hilton Kelliher and Dr. Frances Harris kindly permitted me to consult the recently acquired Trumbull Papers), the Public Record Office, the Warburg Institute, and the Library of the marquess of Bath at Longleat. I am also grateful to the House of Lords Record Office and to Mr. Colin Shrimpton of the Estate Office of Alnwick Castle for answering queries and providing copies of documents.

In addition to general debts to the staff of those institutions, I have incurred a number of particular debts. The earl of Northumberland graciously permitted me to refer to manuscript material in his possession. Dr. Dorothy Johnston and her staff at the Hallward Library kindly allowed me to publish the text of the masque and images of the manuscript containing it. Drs. Lynn Hulse and Ruby Reid Thompson, who were, at the time of the discovery, preparing a catalogue of the literary material in the Portland Papers, assisted with regard to that manuscript. Drs. Martin Butler and James Knowles generously shared with me their own researches on masques from the same period, commented on drafts of the essays underlying this book, and offered many lines of inquiry to pursue. Dr. Stephen Clucas, Professor David Laird, Professor Graham Parry, and Professor Constance Walker likewise commented on drafts of those essays, offering helpful criticisms and suggestions, as did the late Mr. Jeremy Maule, to whose memory this volume is dedicated. Professor Roy Schreiber kindly furnished me with a copy of his monograph on Doncaster; Professor Jackson Bryce assisted with some Latin; and Ms. Susan Wadsworth-Booth was an exemplary editor.

A preliminary report on the discovery of the masque text was presented at a Folger Lunchtime Seminar in February 1996. The members of that seminar offered a number of ideas and pointers; I am especially grateful to Professors Dympna Callaghan, Grace Ioppolo, and James Grantham Turner. Professors Gisèle Venet and François Laroque, and Dr. Line Cottegnies kindly invited me to address their Episteme-IRIS seminar at the University of Paris in March 1998 on the subject of the beauty of the masque.

Finally, Vanessa Laird has contributed more to this work than she knows.

Note on Dates, Transcriptions, and Abbreviations

In the body of the text all dates are given in Old Style, but the year is taken to begin on 1 January. In the notes, in references to documents where confusion might exist (letters sent from the continent and dated both Old and New Style, or documents dated between 1 January and 25 March), both forms are given.

Except where indicated, the following conventions apply to my handling of quotations from seventeenth century texts: the interchangeable letters i/j and u/v are regularized according to modern usage; long and short "s" are not distinguished; brevigraphs and conventional contractions are silently expanded; other abbreviations are expanded in square brackets. Titles of masques by Jonson and Campion are presented in their familiar, modernized forms.

The following abbreviations are employed throughout the work:

BL   British Library

Canova-Green   Marie-Claude Canova-Green. *La politique-specta-cle au grand siècle: les rapports franco-anglais.* Paris, Seattle, and Tübingen: Biblio 17, 1993.

Chamberlain   *The Letters of John Chamberlain.* Ed. Norman Egbert McClure. Memoirs of the American Philosophical Society. Vol. 12. 2 vols. Philadelphia: American Philosophical Society, 1939.

CSPD	*Calendar of State Papers, Domestic Series*
CSPVen.	*Calendar of State Papers, Venetian Series*
DNB	*Dictionary of National Biography*
Ben Jonson	*Ben Jonson.* Ed. C. H. Herford, Percy and Evelyn Simpson. 11 vols. Oxford: Clarendon Press, 1925–52.
HMC	Historical Manuscripts Commission
OED	*Oxford English Dictionary*
Orgel and Strong	Stephen Orgel and Roy Strong. *Inigo Jones: The Theatre of the Stuart Court.* 2 vols. Berkeley and Los Angeles: University of California Press; London: Sotheby Parke Bernet, 1973.
PRO	Public Record Office
Schreiber	Roy E. Schreiber. *The First Carlisle: Sir James Hay, First Earl of Carlisle as Courtier, Diplomat and Entrepreneur, 1580–1636.* Transactions of the American Philosophical Society. Vol. 74, number 7. Philadelphia, 1984.

Text

Textual Introduction

Identification of the Text

The Essex House Masque was danced for the king, the court, and the visiting French ambassador extraordinary on the evening of 8 January 1621 at the London residence of James Hay, Viscount Doncaster.[1] No text for it had been noticed prior to my identification of the anonymous and unidentified manuscript text in the Hallward Library of the University of Nottingham as the libretto for the masque.[2] There are three main areas of evidence for this identification. First, internal evidence provided by the style, theme, tone, and structure of the text suggests that it would have been suitable for performance in so unusual a location and on such an occasion. The same evidence also suggests a connection between this text and the distinctive features of masques associated with Viscount Doncaster. External evidence about the number and identities of the masquers connects the text with the masque and provides a material link between the manuscript and one of the masquers.

Let us begin by considering the evidence provided by the manuscript text itself for the character and date of the masque to which it pertains. Internal evidence affords reason for regarding the text as a mature Jacobean production designed for a private house entertainment of some dignity. The restrained yet confident employment of two antimasques points to the period following the appearance of the double antimasque in 1617 and preceding the proliferation of antimasques in the early 1630s.[3] The small number of performers required by the text (around 18 in all, with no more than 10 on stage at one time) and the rudimentary, even hackneyed scenic devices implied by it (an opening cave and a rock) point to limitations on space, and are thus more suggestive of a private house entertainment than a masque at court. But the refined tone and elevated subject matter of the masque text, which concerns itself with the lawful conduct of love, are far removed from the bawdy of private house entertainments like the *Gypsies Metamorphosed*, suggesting an occasion of some consequence. The text is, in fact, very close in scale, theme, tone—and, as we shall soon see, structure—to another masque offered by Viscount Doncaster to a French ambassador: Ben Jonson's *Lovers Made Men* (1617). Finally, an apparent reference in the first antimasque to *Pan's Anniversary* (an allusion discussed at length in chapter 2, below: "Politics") seems to locate the masque in the festive season of 1620–21. So much, then, for the internal evidence, which suggests a masque of the appropriate character, tone, and shape for performance at Essex House in January 1621.

If we set the newly discovered text in the context of those masques known to have been sponsored by Viscount Doncaster, and those over which his tastes might have exerted some influence, we find that it has a decidedly Doncastrian tang.[4] The text is distinguished both by its call for the doubling-up of masquers as antimasquers and by its use of metamorphosis as the means of effecting the change from one state to the other. This is a highly unusual conceit, paralleled in this precise fashion only, perhaps, in *Lovers Made Men*. I am not claiming that the metamorphosis of antimasquers— distinctive though it is—is exclusively associated with Doncaster: we find it in the petrifaction of the rebels in *The Golden Age Restored*, for instance. We also find the emergence of masquers from a state of gracelessness in *Lord Hay's Masque*, in which trees are turned (or, in fact, *re*turned) to men, and in *The Lords' Masque*, in which statues are animated. In the *Irish Masque at Court*, moreover, a group of Irish ambassadors are anglicized. And in *The Gypsies Metamorphosed* the marquess of Buckingham and his fellow vagabonds are "turned into" courtiers; so are a group of rebel spirits in a contemporaneous masque discovered by James Knowles.[5] Metamorphoses are not unknown; but only very rarely do we find a transformation of antimasquers into masquers. The antimasquers who threaten the Golden Age are petrified and remain that way; the dancing trees of *Lord Hay's* and the inanimate statues of *The Lords' Masque* perform no antimasque; nor do the Irish ambassadors at court, who dance a most dignified entry. (The trees do dance, however, and clearly approach the condition of antimasquers; perhaps Doncaster's influence may be detected here, for *Lord Hay's Masque* was commissioned to celebrate his marriage of 1607—he was also heavily involved in the production of *The Lords' Masque* in 1613.) The transformation of antimasquers into masquers in both *The Gypsies Metamorphosed* and the other masque from the same period and milieu suggests less the commonplace character of the conceit than its temporary modishness in the wake of *Lovers Made Men* (as is argued in chapter 2, below: "Consequences"). The transformation of antimasquers into masquers is, then, a distinctive conceit that buttresses those similarities of theme, scale, and tone that appear to link the newly discovered text with the highly distinctive *Lovers Made Men*.

The transformation of antimasquers into masquers is only one of the Doncastrian signatures found in the newly discovered text; the use of nine masquers is another. Nine men appeared in *Lord Hay's Masque*, and nine women, among them Doncaster's wife, were to have appeared in the cancelled *Masque of Amazons* in 1618.[6] I am not suggesting that the use of nine masquers was exclusive to Doncaster, merely that it was an unusual number for a group of masquers and was often employed by him.[7] The intersection of these two signatures in the newly discovered text, in which nine masquers are transformed, as they were in his wedding masque, further encourages us to associate the new text with Doncaster.

Internal evidence has suggested that the manuscript text has a broadly Doncastrian flavor; external evidence provides firm links between that text and the Essex House performance. The most important source for identifying the text is Sir John Finett, who mentions the masque at Essex House in his memoirs, referring to it as "a Maske presented by nine young Gentlemen, whereof the Lord *Montjoy*, and a Son of the Lord *Hollis* were two &c."[8] Our first point of departure is Finett's note that "nine young Gentlemen" presented the masque. We have observed that nine is an unusual number of masquers and that it was favored by Doncaster; we have noticed also that the newly discovered text is for a masque of nine and that these figures must be transformed from antimasquers into masquers: I want now to suggest that these performers *must* have been nine young gentlemen. The text calls for the transformation of nine rebellious Giants, newly born of Tellus, into nine attractive and well-mannered youths, animated by Prometheus. The wild antimasque of lusty young Giants would have been unsuitable for mature and dignified courtiers to dance, and the masque, revealing a youthful "spring of man," would have been inappropriate either for such courtiers on the one hand or for professional actors on the other. Nine young gentlemen, and nine young gentlemen only, would therefore have been suited to the performance of the newly discovered text. This deduction adds considerable weight to the internal evidence already presented for associating the newly discovered text with Doncaster: it provides a precise connection between the manuscript text and *The Essex House Masque.*

Finally, although Finett's allusion to the identities of these gentlemen is maddeningly contracted, valuable information can nonetheless be gleaned from it. Finett identifies one of the masquers as a son of "Lord *Hollis*"—John Holles, Lord Haughton, that is. He thus provides a material link between the manuscript text and one of the masquers: the following section of this introduction shows that the newly discovered text appears in a manuscript compiled by the Holles family historian, a member of the family who was, moreover, resident in the household of "Lord *Hollis*" at the time his son danced in the masque.[9] The existence of such a link would not, in itself, be conclusive; but the bridges afforded by Finett, which link the text with the masque and the manuscript with one of the masquers, buttress the stylistic and structural evidence already advanced for associating the newly discovered text with Viscount Doncaster. Taken together, this evidence allows us to identify the manuscript text as the libretto for *The Essex House Masque* of 1621.

The Manuscript

The text of the masque appears in a small manuscript volume containing a holograph version of a history of the Holles family by Gervase Holles (1607–75), a young cousin of John Holles, first earl of Clare.[10] The manuscript currently resides among the Portland Papers in the Hallward Library of Nottingham University, where it is catalogued as Pw V 6. The manuscript is a composite volume, consisting of what appear at some point to have been three separate quarto booklets bound up together: the masque appears in the last of these.[11] These booklets appear to have been the working notebooks, or "table books," of Gervase Holles, in which he assembled family materials, and jotted drafts of poems and notes for his history. The first contains notes and jottings in Holles's hand, together with a draft of his family history, the *Memorials*; it also includes a copy (in another hand) of an elegy on John Skeffington (a relative on Holles's mother's side) by John Cade—a poem composed in 1613. The middle section of the manuscript contains an additional chapter of the *Memorials* in Holles's hand; and the final section is a small literary miscellany, including the text of the masque (fols. 108v–12v), an excerpt from John Vaughan's "Elegie" (fol. 112v), incomplete texts of Donne's first three "Satyrs" (fols. 115r–19v), "Oberons Pallace by R[obert] H[errick]" (fol. 120r), and a poem in Holles's hand entitled, "In my Study" (fol. 121r). These pieces were probably transcribed in the 1630s, when Holles began to assemble materials pertaining to his family history. Such a date is supported by the circulation profile of the literary items with no family connection: the Herrick and Donne poems, for instance, appear to have circulated in manuscript from the 1620s through the 1640s, with a particular concentration in the 1630s. Further confirmation for this view is provided by the fact that on the verso of the leaf containing the Herrick poem (fol. 120v), Holles has jotted notes on the earl of Strafford and his death (12 May 1641).

There are apparently three hands at work in this last section of the manuscript, in addition to that of Holles: the Donne poems are in one hand (D), while the remaining works are in another hand (B), with the exception of the central section of the masque (lines 50–87), which is in yet another hand (C). B is a small, neat, running italic with a pronounced slope to the right; it incorporates certain secretary features, such as majuscule "C" and reversed "e." Distinguishing features include the descender on the "f," which is frequently looped to the right, giving the letter the appearance of an elongated "t" (figure 1). It also features clubbed ascenders and descenders. C is a larger, more upright italic, with some secretary features. It is naive in appearance, and is typified by fat loops on ascenders (figure 2). The two scripts do not appear to be the products of a single hand.

It looks from the layout of the page as though Gervase Holles himself was responsible for overseeing the transcription of the masque. Holles habitually made use of servants, friends, and relatives to prepare copies of documents for his family historical collections. In overseeing their work he consistently set up the paper for writing in a distinctive fashion: in order to create a guide line for the wide lefthand margin he favored, he folded each leaf three times along the vertical to create four equally-sized panels measuring 35mm across. His method of folding was consistent: the outer fold went one way and the two inner folds the opposite way. The paper is folded in this fashion throughout the text of the *Memorials* (fols. 9–64), and at several other points in the manuscript. At such points, it is fair to assume that Holles oversaw the preparation of the paper, and reasonable to infer that he was responsible for securing the transcription of the items there copied. Although hands B and C cannot be identified, the folds in folios 108–12 seem to suggest that Holles prepared the leaves for transcription. He evidently instructed the first scribe (B) to follow his use of the guide line for a wide left hand margin (here 25–32mm): B did so on folios 108v (lines 1–17; figure 1) and 109r (lines 18–49), and C, taking over at the top of folio 109v, followed him in copying lines 50–87 (figure 2 shows lines 50–74; the margins here are slightly narrower than normal, due to cropping of the paper). At the top of folio 110r (line 75), however, C neglected to set up the paper in this fashion, using a rough, narrow left margin (14mm). When B took over halfway down the page (line 88) he followed C's lead and retained the narrow

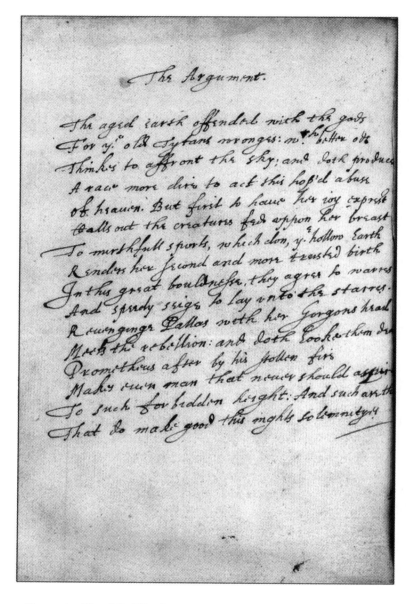

Figure 1   Hand B, *The Essex House Masque*; Pw V 6, fol. 108v
(lines 1–17). Reproduced by permission of the Hallward Library,
University of Nottingham.

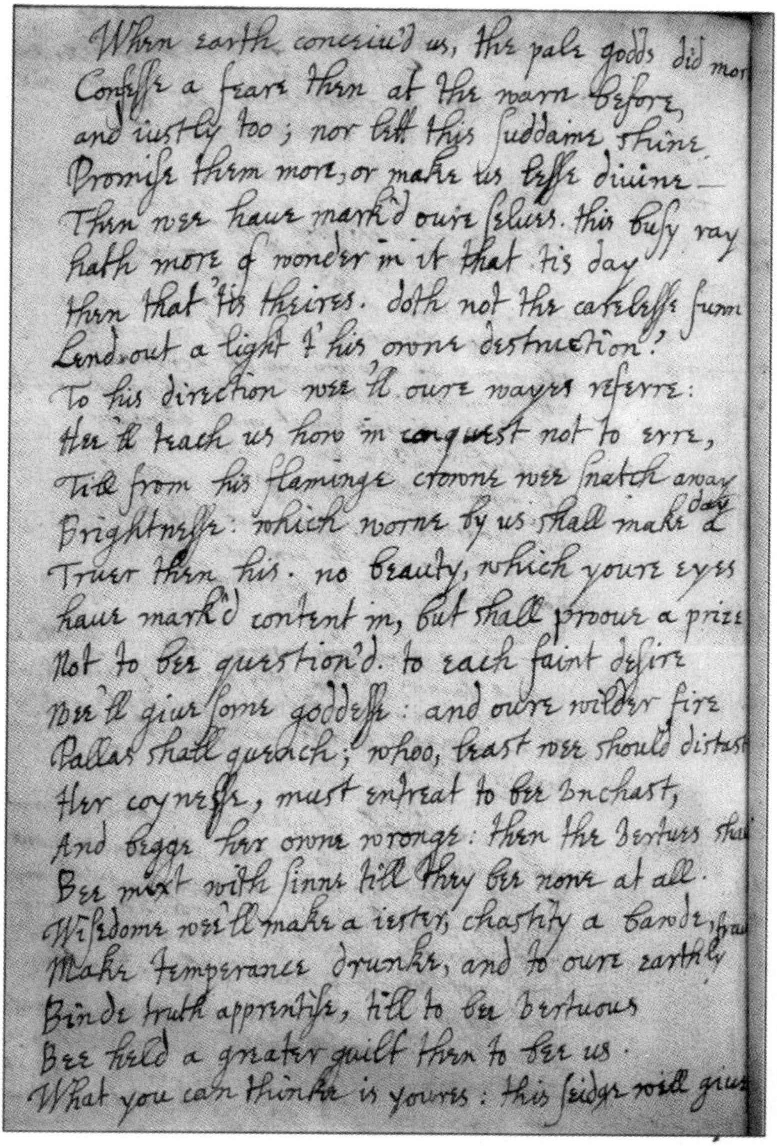

Figure 2 Hand C, *The Essex House Masque*; Pw V 6, fol. 109v
(lines 50–74). Reproduced by permission of the Hallward Library,
University of Nottingham.

margin. He also retained it at the top of folio 110v (line 98; 10–18mm), but (realizing his error) gradually widened the margin as he wrote, until it reached the guide line. He retained the wide margin at the top of folio 111r (line 124; 33mm), but slipped back to the left after an indented stage direction near the bottom of the page (19mm). From thence he continued to work close to the left margin (fols 111v–12r; lines 156, 190; 10–15mm) until the final page (fol. 112v; line 217), where he widened the margin once again for the final lines of the masque (17mm), but reverted to the narrow margin for the first lines of the hastily copied "Elegie." This pattern of work is confirmed by the distribution of transcriptional errors in the text. B's first portion is carefully laid out and largely error-free; C's portion of the text, while not laid out according to Holles's instructions, is likewise almost entirely free of errors. After B's return to transcription, however, the quality of work deteriorates. Errors include the incorporation of redundant letters, the omission of letters, the misplacement of material, and the omission of entire words. In one case the scribe even fails to notice his error (line 111).[12]

Although it is impossible to determine for certain why the masque text appears in Pw V 6, its appearance without ascription or indication of its occasion implies that it was copied for someone who was well aware of its significance.[13] Given the character of the other items bound in Pw V 6 and the use of the latter part of this section of the manuscript for notes relating to the Holles family, the most obvious explanation for its inclusion is that it was transcribed for Gervase Holles because he was aware of its family interest. Gervase would have known about *The Essex House Masque* because one of his cousins appeared in it while he was resident in the household of the first earl of Clare.[14] The character of the text, furthermore, suggests that it was taken either from a performance text or some sort of informal souvenir copy, rather than from a retrospective account, carefully prepared for presentation, publication, or other dissemination:[15] it lacks the detailed descriptions and explications typical of the latter (as, for instance, in Jonson's manuscript text of *The Masque of Queens*); stage directions are fairly brief, are given in the present tense, and fail to offer intelligible accounts of such critical junctures as the main masque; finally, as will be shown below, the text is punctuated to guide a speaker, rather than a reader. It may well be, then, that the source of Gervase Holles's text was his cousin, the masquer.[16]

Editorial Procedure

My goal has been to produce an accurate edition of the text for students of the court masque. Since such students are unlikely to be unduly troubled by seventeenth century conventions, modernization did not seem necessary. The open question of authorship, moreover, made it desirable to preserve as much evidence of the character of the manuscript as was consistent with readability. Since a semidiplomatic edition is already available, I have not attempted to reflect every formal detail of the manuscript; I have rather sought to dress the text appropriately for an appearance in print, making changes only when they seemed absolutely necessary to avoid confusion, and striving for a balance between clarity and fidelity.

Only three substantive emendations were necessary: first, the provision of a title, which I have placed in square brackets; second, the insertion of the verb "have" (also in square brackets) in line 111, on the grounds that it was evidently omitted by the copyist; and, third, the expansion of the abbreviated direction "Tell: son:" in line 21.

I have altered the orthography of the text a little. The letters u/v and i/j are distinguished according to modern practice; long "s" is transcribed simply as "s." The following conventional contractions are silently expanded: "-cōn" for

"-cion," "-mᵗ." for "-ment," "Mʳˢ." for "Mistress," "wᶜʰ." for "which," "wᵗʰ." for "with," "yᵉ." for "the," "yᵒʳ." for "your," and "yᵗ" for "that." In regard to capitalization, I have attempted to bring the text into line with the system employed but not uniformly adhered to in the manuscript. In common with contemporary practice, the manuscript capitalizes most initial letters in lines of verse, along with the names of deities, animals, personifications, and technical terms (cosmological, legal, or governmental).[17] Although I have not sought to impose complete consistency on the text, I have intervened in the most distracting cases of failure to follow this system, silently capitalizing initial letters in lines of verse or stage directions, and two uncapitalized proper names ("venus" and "mars"; lines 164, 165). I have also tempered scribe B's eccentric tendency to capitalize all instances of initial "A," reducing to lowercase the indefinite article in lines 34, 35, 101, 108, 112, 114, 125, 153, 176, and 186.[18]

The manuscript exhibits a coherent and rhetorically helpful system of punctuation, designed to help an actor deliver the lines; I have altered it only when I thought it necessary to prevent confusion. In practice this means that I have emended only where errors or inconsistencies were apparent, or where the system itself looked likely to bewilder even a modern reader used to working with early modern conventions. Periods are silently inserted at the ends of songs, stanzas, or speeches; all other changes are noted in the Emendations of Accidentals. Virgules are removed on the grounds that they were not usually preserved in print;[19] periods replace solitary virgules at the ends of speeches, songs, or stage directions. Question marks replace periods or semicolons where their absence is likely to mislead a modern reader, used to seeing interrogatives so registered. While the speeches are governed by the pointing system outlined below, the songs, by contrast, are barely punctuated at all; I have, as far as possible, left them that way.

With regard to the layout of the text I have readily intervened. To make the masque as clear as possible for the reader, stage directions and speech headings are centered and placed in italics, without regard for their positioning in the manuscript. Catchwords, deletions, corrections, and interlineations are not shown, and folio numbers are not recorded. Readers interested in these and other formal features of the manuscript may consult the semidiplomatic edition printed in my article "The 'Lost' *Essex House Masque*" (101–09).

A Note on Punctuation

In common with other dramatic texts of the period, the punctuation of the manuscript—especially that of its speeches—is rhetorical rather than logical or syntactic: it is designed to help a speaker follow the contours of the verse.[20] Punctuation marks thus tend not to mark off grammatical members, but to guide delivery, indicating pauses of different lengths for stress, balance, and suspense. Several marks appear, the precise value of which can only be determined by an assessment of their context.[21] A number of general observations might, however, be useful to a reader approaching the text for the first time.

Four marks, used with comparable frequency, comprise the core system: the period or full stop, the colon, the semicolon, and the comma. Generally speaking, these points represent a hierarchy of pauses, from the heaviest (the period) to the lightest (the comma). Perhaps the most surprising feature of this system to a modern reader is its occasional use of the period followed by an uncapitalized letter to register a pause within rather than the completion of a sentence. This was a convention of the age: a little old-fashioned, perhaps, but unexceptionable.[22] I have left such uses intact because, once understood, the practice presents no real problems, and because to modernize in this instance would either create serious inconsistencies or lead to the repointing of the entire text—a project that seems to me both unnecessary and undesirable.

The colon indicates a lighter pause than a period and often introduces supplementary, parallel, or antithetical clauses. Its employment frequently tallies with modern usage, but it is often deployed either more lightly—where we would use a comma—or more emphatically—where we might use a period. The semicolon is likewise used for emphasis, suspense, and balance, but registers a slightly lighter pause than the colon. Colons and semicolons are occasionally used to underscore the caesura when the syllabic configuration makes it difficult for a speaker to register a pause, as when a terminal sibilant immediately precedes the caesura (lines 48, 74, 116, 169).[23] Such usage looks, at first glance, rather heavy-handed; once one understands what it is trying to communicate, it is quite helpful to a speaker.

The comma marks a very light pause, sometimes merely indicating that the speaker should draw breath; on one occasion it encloses a short phrase which might—due to a surrounding cluster of consonants—trip up an unwary speaker (line 159).

Other marks used intermittently are the question mark, hyphen, and exclamation mark. The question mark presents no problems (although, as noted above, I have added some of them for clarity). The hyphen is used once, to prevent a speaker pausing at a line ending where the desired enjambment is not obvious (line 53). On one occasion (line 106), a mark that appears to be an exclamation mark (but which might also be read as a question mark, or an inverted—though here, more precisely, "reversed"—semicolon) indicates a stress and pause in order to establish an antithesis.[24] Finally, an unpunctuated line ending generally implies a light pause, unless an enjambment is implied or indicated.

The system thus described is not a modern one; but it has its own logic and its own advantages: it allows for a degree of flexibility in the syntax, yielding frequently productive ambiguities that modernization would pin down and erase. It also has an inherent interest as a guide to the actual delivery of the text in performance.

[The Essex House Masque]

The Argument.

The aged earth offended with the gods
For the old Tytans wronges: with better ods
Thinkes to affront the sky; and doth produce
A race more dire to act this hop'd abuse
Of heaven. But first to have her joy exprest
Calls out the creatures fed uppon her breast
To mirthfull sports, which don, the hollow Earth
Renders her second and more trusted birth.
In this great bouldnesse, they agree to warres   10
And speedy seige to lay unto the starres.
Revenginge Pallas with her Gorgons head
Meets the rebellion: and doth looke them dead.
Prometheus after by his stollen fire
Makes even man that never should aspire
To such forbidden height: And such are these
That do make good this nights solemnityes.

First is sunge this followinge song, supposed to be don by
the earth that summons her creatures to rejoyce at the hope
of her revenge.   20

Tellus song 1. The glad Earth summons to appeare
                 All those whom she doth foster heare
                 And such cheerefull lookes to bringe
                 As if minted by the springe.
                 The spreadinge tree, not urg'd by charmes
                 Must seeme t'have feet as well as armes.
                 The mynes of mocion must pertake
                 Which neyther growth nor earthquake make.
                 The Lyon grimme must not gainesay
                 To daunce, allthough he want his prey.   30
                 The nymble Ape, the sober sheepe,
                 The Boare, the stag; must help to keep
                 This gladsom revell: now wee pay
                 For our revenge a hollyday.

The Antemaskers beinge calld out by the songe, fall into a
daunce, which don, they presently vanish, and the cave
appeares, from whence issue .9. giants the supposed sonnes
and champions of the earth, warlikely arrayed; where of one
speakes.

Gyant. Great Birth of earth, the suffringe world to you   40
         Offers her cause; nor is the greivance new
         Which beggs her accion: But such as the might
         Of the fam'd Tytans undertooke to right
         Yet faintly fayld of: let it not bee said
         Our mothers issue made the gods affraid
         And could no more; for vengance wee were meant
         And hate was mingled with our nourishment
         To them and all their lawes: our nature's ill

Nor have wee fed on ought but what would kill.
When earth conceiv'd us, the pale godds did more   50
Confesse a feare then at the warre before,
And justly too; nor lett this suddaine shine
Promise them more, or make us lesse divine–
Then wee have mark'd oure selves. this busy ray
Hath more of wonder in it that tis day
Then that 'tis theires. doth not the carelesse sunn
Lend out a light t'his owne destruction?
To his direction wee'll oure wayes referre:
Hee'll teach us how in conquest not to erre,
Till from his flaminge crowne wee snatch away   60
Brightnesse: which worne by us shall make a day
Truer then his. no beauty, which youre eyes
Have mark'd content in, but shall proove a prize
Not to bee question'd. To each faint desire
Wee'll give some goddesse: and oure wilder fire
Pallas shall quench; whoo, least wee should distast
Her coynesse, must entreat to bee unchast,
And begge her owne wronge: then the vertues shall
Bee mixt with sinne till they bee none at all.
Wisedome wee'll make a jester, chastity a bawde,   70
Make temperance drunke, and to our earthly fraud
Binde truth apprentise, till to bee vertuous
Bee held a greater guilt then to bee us.
What you can thinke is youres: this seidge will give
All by which immortality doth live.
Oure strength wee have about us, and no want
Of armes, unlesse oure mother earth bee scant:
Whome wee will hurle at Jove; if hee reply,
His thunder shall returne his destiny:
Proppt by her aged shoulders then wee'll rise   80
Till wee have made the starrs Antipodes.
This glory to secure, with one consent
Lett's trace a terrour to the firmament.

This done they fall into a warrelike dance which is per-
formed to loud musicke, they after fall of by degrees, and
clime to theire places, where settlinge themselves Pallas
enters, and veiwinge them:

Thus I locke up your madnesse: doth the hand
Of heaven and us obey the soft command
So oft of mercy, to let sin growe high,   90
Enough to dare against infinity?
Could not the punishment of those first proud
Rebells; obtaine to have our power allow'd
Mightier then earthes? or thought these that the skarrs
Disabled heaven had in the former warres?
Are gods so lowe condicion'd: not to bee
Or knowne or feard; but by their Tyranny
And angry warninges? twice was heaven assayld
Chac'te from her selfe; and dyety in vayld
In some lowe shape; which it before had made   100
But with a carelesse hand: Nature againe
Did allmost tremble for her soveraigne
Callinge for soddaine reskue: yet did wee shun
Vengance; expectinge when bold sin would run
Into repentance; and confesse the stay
Of fate not to bee weakenesse! but delay.
Till care of all these Glories which appeare
The least of which is worth a Goddesse feare
Call'd us to shew them death, and make them learne
By punishment that power to discerne   110
Which goodnesse should [have] taught: nor was our fight
Vantadg'd with other weapon then a sight
Where Fate lay lodg'd, whose ev'ry killing nod
Cut of daunger from a troubled god.
Returninge Earth her one. who may this
Score of her sorrowes: count her fruitfullnes.

Fastned to shame wee leave them; and entreat
Each starre to call into their former seat
Their frighted colours: and to shine agen
Not cold; and carelessly; but so as when   120
You courted Nature in your youth; and gave
Thankfull aspects for those faire lookes you have.

This ended Pallas departs; immediately this song is sunge:

Song .2. Such be his ruine that can find
           So foule a thought about his mind
           As the pleasure to conceave;
           Without the comfort of a leave
           Which beauty parts with: may he die
           Sentenc'd by that beautyes eie.
           And more uggly grone till shee   130
           Confesse the change is worse then hee.
           Heaven and beauty are allied:
           Both are with like wonder spied;
           Both serv'd alike too: and the way
           To win eyther is to pray.
           Course attempts are here deni'de
           But such courtship as the Bride
           Makes to her thoughts; when shee would faine
           Call to mind her lovers vaine
           Is here admitted: if you try   140
           Rougher waies to gaine her by
               Each motion from your Mistress' face
               Is execution and not grace.

This song ended Prometheus enters with his fire supposed
to be stollen from heaven: and speakes as followeth.

Veiw this begettinge flame; wherein the age
To come is ready: see the parentage
Of all that must bee man: filch't by this hand
When all the gods the robbery did withstand.
With choysest care commandinge every eye   150
Of Argus to reveale the Theevery.
Strange subtlety of fire. not such whereby
Cold nature warmes her; but a mistery
Of heat made up so pure; that it can try
The elements; and hath no contrary
But death; tis lifes matereall, temper'd so
By skillfull handlinge, that it can bestow
All the affections nature owes, nor are
Any ingredients, in't, that heaven could spare.
The sparkles of the morninge: stollen from   160
Carelesse Apollo at his nightly home,
Are here together put: with some addition
There to imparted from the lamp of noone;
The lusting lookes of Venus, by which shee
Intreated Mars first to Adultery,
Are caught in this; and for allay; the chast
Light of the winter moone, is with them plac'd.
The fire of comets, such as do appeare
More to the Artists; then the peoples feare,
Higher then Aire hath place; met with the light   170
Snatch'd from the thunderbolts amazinge flight.
The beautious starres coole shooting; cunningly
Mingled, with sparkes of Junoes Jealousy
Make up this lamp of life: by which we can
Deale soule into cold stone, and raise up man
Out of a punishment with moderate heat
Such as wise nature fancies. I'le beget
Obedient life; and manners so refine
As may discover that to be divine

Which lent them shape and beeinge: skillfully   180
Recov'ringe so my ruin'd auncestry
From out this stony judgment. who shall wake
Pleasures to those they frighted; and nere take
A thought of Roughnes. But the life I give
Shall weare in servinge you by whom I live
Divinest powers. spare a saving glaunce
This worke of life to reskue; if mischaunce
Dare to attempt it, daunger: and be due
Onely to me the Art, the thankes to you.

This ended Prometheus departs with his fire, and this song   190
is forthwith heard.

    Calmely looke and with desire
        Ad to the fire
    Which your breathinges must fan higher
        Life to renew:
        For all the art
        Cannot impart
    So much thereof as you.

    To close an eye be not about
        For past all doubt   200
    At ev'ry winke: a life's put out
        And you'rs th'offence
        Since ev'ry sparke
        That is so darke
    Must be supplied from thence.

The discovery of the maine maske is made uppon the singing
of this verse:

Then veiw the spring of man begun
   By your one sun
Which in smyles his course doth run.   210
   And then if one
   Mong'st all you find
   That is unkind
Know he was made of stone.

The discovery beinge made the maskers daunce, which
ended this songe invites them to the Ladyes.

Let each man to his wonder move
In footing made by none but love:
   Tis heart
   No art   220
Must this motion frame and shee
Her selfe must be the harmony.

Then gently dwell uppon her hand
Yet so that she may understand
   Her touch
   Is such
That it can urge the fire anewe
To kindle that was spent in you.

Pace then forth but let your walke
Woo as kindly as your talke: 230
   A paire
   Like aire
Fillinge each place with swift supply
Where musicke threatens vacancy.

Finis.

Emendations of Accidentals

9	birth.] ~∧		113	lodg'd,] ~∧
13	dead.] ~∧		116	fruitfullnes.] ~∧
17	solemnityes.] ~./		123	*departs;*] ~∧
20	revenge] ~./		123	*sunge:*] ~:/
24	springe.] ~∧		132	allied:] ~∧
26	armes.] ~∧		133	spied;] ~∧
28	make.] ~∧		143	grace.] ~/
30	prey.] ~∧		145	*heaven:*] ~.
32	keep] ~.		169	feare,] ~∧
34	hollyday.] ~./		171	flight.] ~∧
38	*earth,*] ~;		191	*heard.*] ~./
38	*arrayed;*] ~∧		195	renew:] ~∧
39	*speakes.*] ~./		198	you.] ~./
49	kill.] ~∧		205	thence.] ~./
77	scant:] ~.		207	*verse:*] ~/
87	*them:*] ~∧		216	*Ladyes.*] ~./
91	infinity?] ~.		218	love:] ~∧
95	warres?] ~.		230	talke:] ~∧
98	warninges?] ~;		234	vacancy.] ~/

Commentary

1–5   *aged . . . heaven*: cf. Claudian, *Gigantomachia*, lines 1–5, and Apollodorus, *The Library*, 1.6.1.

8   *mirthfull sports*: An allusion to *The Kings Majesties Declaration to His Subjects Concerning lawfull Sports to be used* (London, 1618), and to the phrase "*honest mirth*" which appears therein (4).

12–13   *Revenginge . . . rebellion*: cf. Claudian, *Gigantomachia*, lines 91–93.

21   *The glad Earth*: cf. Thomas Campion, *Lord Hay's Masque* (1607), note on Zephirus "the glad earth"; *The Works of Thomas Campion*, ed. Walter R. Davis (New York: Doubleday, 1967; London: Faber, 1969), 216, note 24. (All quotations from the masques of Campion are taken from this edition; references are to page numbers.)

25–26   *tree . . . armes*: cf. Ovid, *Metamorphoses*, 10.86–105; Campion, *Lord Hay's Masque*: "Earth, then be soft and passable to free | These fettered roots!" (220)

27   *mynes*: apparently subterranean cavities, rather than earthworks to extract minerals (*OED, sb.* 1.d), as the following line urges that the motion to be undertaken by the mines should *not* involve the generation of minerals.

27   *mocion*: cf. Ben Jonson, *Mercury Vindicated from the Alchemists* (1615): "*Nature* is motions mother" (line 242; quotations from and references to the works of Jonson follow the text of *Ben Jonson* and are cited by line number only). For the mechanics of mines in motion, cf. the revelation of a gold mine in *The Memorable Masque* of George Chapman and Inigo Jones (1613), [Description], lines 114–20, 157–60; ed. G. Blakemore Evans, in *The Plays of George Chapman. The Comedies: A Critical Edition*, gen. ed. Allan Holaday (Urbana, Chicago, and London: University of Illinois Press, 1970). (All quotations from and references to *The Memorable Masque* or Chapman's comedies follow this edition.)

28   *growth*: Metals were thought to grow in the earth, through the power of the sun.

28   *earthquake*: According to Aristotle, earthquakes were caused by windy exhalations of earth generated by the heat of the sun and trapped in subterranean caverns; Aristotle, *Meteorologica*, 365b 21; S. K. Heninger, Jr., *A Handbook of Renaissance Meteorology* (Durham, N. C.: Duke University Press, 1960), 128–34.

29   *Lyon grimme*: The grimness of lions was legendary: cf. Shakespeare, "the grim lion," *The Rape of Lucrece* (1609), line 421. For the possible appearance of the lion, see figure 3.

31   *nymble Ape*: Apes were notoriously agile and cunning: see Pliny, *Natural History*, 8.80.215. For the possible appearance of the ape, see figure 4. Apes had earlier appeared in *The Memorable Masque* of Chapman and Jones (see "The Presentment," lines 163–65), and in Francis Beaumont's *Masque of The Inner Temple* (1613).

31   *sober sheepe*: A witty play on the common notion that sheep seldom drink; Edward Topsell, *A Historie of Foure-footed Beastes* (London, 1607), 605.

32   *Boare*: A symbol of lust.

32   *stag*: One of the gentlest of animals: see Pliny, *Natural History*, 8.50.112

34   *For our revenge a hollyday*: cf. Jonson, *Pan's Anniversary* (1621): "*This is the Shepherds Holy-day*" (lines 10, 24; cf. also line 17). Jonson's phrase, with its etymological spelling designed to emphasize the sacredness of the occasion, is mocked here.

35   *Antemaskers*: cf. the antimasque of beasts in *The Lords' Masque* of Campion and Jones (1613); Andrew J. Sabol, ed., *A Score for* The Lords' Masque *by Thomas Campion* (Hanover and London: University Press of New England, 1993), 24–25, 326–27. Five species of beast appear (on nature's tendency to do things by fives, see Plutarch, *Moralia*, 439F–430A).

35   *Antemaskers*: See figure 5, and discussion below, pages 121, 122.

36–37   *cave appeares*: One of the hoariest of masque devices, as Chapman's Plutus noted at the opening of *The Memorable*

Figure 3 Inigo Jones, Lion; from *Tempe Restored* (1632).
Reproduced by permission of the Chatsworth Settlement Trustees.

Figure 4 Inigo Jones, Ape; from *Tempe Restored* (1632).
Reproduced by permission of the Chatsworth Settlement Trustees.

Figure 5 Inigo Jones, Animal-headed antimasquers (*c.* 1620).
Reproduced by permission of the Chatsworth Settlement Trustees.

                      Masque, "The Presentment," lines 3–13: see Orgel and
Strong, numbers 13, 46, 60–63, 146; Enid Welsford, *The Court
Masque: A Study in the Relationship between Poetry &
the Revels* (Cambridge: Cambridge University Press, 1927),
162–65, 181, 193, 206, 241, 286; and discussion below, pages
125–27.

40–83   *Great . . . firmament*: Cf. Claudian, *Gigantomachia*, lines
14–35; Jonson and Jones, *The Golden Age Restored* (1616),
lines 30–65.

51   *then*: than. The two terms were more or less interchangeable (*OED*); "then" is used throughout the masque.

52   *shine*: brightness; *OED, sb.*[1] 1.a.

63   *prize*: "Anything seized or captured by force, especially in
war"; *OED, sb.*[3] 2.a.

64–67   *each . . . unchast*: cf. Claudian, *Gigantomachia*, lines 40–
41.

77–78   *unlesse . . . Jove*: cf. Claudian, *Gigantomachia*, line 29.

81   *Till . . . Antipodes*: cf. Claudian, *Gigantomachia*, lines 31–32.

83   *trace*: tread (*OED, v.*¹ I.4); dance (*OED, v.*¹ I.2); also mark (*OED, v.*¹ III.9).

86   *clime to theire places*: The antimasquers leave the dance and ascend the stage or scene, in preparation for their "locking up" by Pallas. Cf. Chapman and Jones, *The Memorable Masque*, [Description], lines 112–13.

86–87   *Pallas enters*: cf. Jonson and Jones, *The Golden Age Restored*, lines 66–83. For the conventional appearance of Pallas, see figure 6. For other appearances by Pallas in contemporary masques and entertainments, see Samuel Daniel, *The Vision of the Twelve Goddesses* (1604); Thomas Middleton and William Rowley, *A Courtly Masque: The Device, called The World tost at Tennis* (1619–20); Middleton, *Speech intended for the generall Training*, in *Honorable Entertainments* (1621).

88   *Thus . . . madnesse*: cf. Claudian, *Gigantomachia*, lines 91–128; figure 7.

98   *twice*: first by the Titans; then by the Giants.

99–100   *dyety . . . shape*: According to some versions of the legend, after the assault of the Giants, the gods fled to Egypt and took on the shapes of animals; see Natalis Comes, *Natalis Comitis Mythologiæ sive Explicationum Fabularum Libri X* (Venice, 1581), 6.21; George Sandys, *Ovid's Metamorphosis Englished, Mythologiz'd, and Represented in Figures*, ed. Karl K. Hulley and Stanley T. Vandersall (Lincoln, Nebr.: University of Nebraska Press, 1970), 250–51.

103   *soddaine*: sudden (obsolete form of); *OED*.

106   *weaknesse!*: The punctuation mark in the manuscript here is ambiguous: it might possibly be a question mark or an inverted (or, strictly speaking, reversed) semicolon. An exclamation mark would, however, most aptly register both a suspensory pause and the emphasis required to bring out the antithesis between "weakness" and "delay."

Figure 6   Inigo Jones, Statue of Pallas (*c.* 1618). Reproduced by permission of the Chatsworth Settlement Trustees.

104   *PICTA*
STVPOR ADMIRATIONIS, EX
ARMORVM,& LITERARVM
PRAESTANTIA.

INDITA BELLONAE *Sapientia,& arma Minervæ*
Gorgonis os clypeo quæ gerit anguicomum
Vertit,& hoc monstro homines in saxa rigentes
Cernere tale oculis qui voluêre caput.
SCIRE *cupis quid significet Panoplia talis*
Pallados armatæ, monstriferæque Deæ?
LITTERAE & ARMA(*quibus Sapiētia,palmaq̃,victrix*
Quæritur)hæc duo sunt inclyta præcipuè:
Quorum homines rapit admiratiotanta:stupore
Defixos,vt eos saxa quis esse putet.

Figure 7 Pallas with the Gorgon's head, turning men to stone;
from Barthelemy Aneau, *Picta Poesis* (1552). Reproduced by
permission of the British Library.

107   *Glories*: resplendent beauties; *OED*, *sb*. 6.

115   *one*: own (obsolete form of); *OED*.

115–16   *who . . . fruitfullnes*: who may count as her fertility this sum of her grief.

117–22   *entreat . . . aspects*: Pallas's reordering of the heavens would presumably be accompanied by appropriate lighting effects: cf. Campion and Jones, *The Lords' Masque*, 254.

122   *aspects*: An astrological term, denoting the positions of the stars in respect to the earth (*OED*, *sb*. II.4); also, countenances (*OED*, *sb*. III.10). "Thankful" aspects are benevolent.

124–27   *Such . . . leave*: cf. Jean Antoine de Baïf, *Mascarade de Mons. le Duc de Longueville*: "*Six Chevaliers . . . | De six Meduses ont esprouvé les regars: | Ils couvent sous la pierre encor les chaudes larmes*"; *Euvres en Rime de Ian Antoine de Baif*, ed. Ch. Marty-Laveaux, 5 vols. (Paris, 1881–90), 2:338.

127   *leave*: permission; *OED*, 1.a.

128   *parts with*: surrenders, yields; *OED*, II.6.c.

132   *Heaven and beauty are allied*: A central tenet of Platonic thought: see Plato, *Phaedrus*, 250; *Symposium*, 209b–212a; cf. Plotinus, *Enneads*, 1.6.1; 5.8.3; Marsilio Ficino, *De Amore*, 2.3 (all citations refer to the translation by Sears Jayne, *Commentary on Plato's Symposium on Love* [Dallas: Spring, 1985]).

144   *Prometheus enters*: cf. Campion and Jones, *The Lords' Masque*, 252ff; Jonson and Jones, *Mercury Vindicated*, lines 196ff. For the tableau implied here, see figure 8. For the conventional presentation of the stolen fire, see figure 9.

146–77   *Veiw . . . fancies*: cf. Apollodorus, *The Library*, 1.7.1.

148   *filch't*: stolen, or taken surreptitiously; *OED*, *v*. 1.

152–55   *Strange . . . elements*: the celestial, elemental fire—fountain of life, purifier, and source of motion—as opposed to the material, sublunary fire; see Marsilio Ficino, *Three Books on Life*, ed. and trans. Carol V. Kaske and John R. Clark (Binghamton, N. Y.: Medieval & Renaissance Texts & Studies, 1989), 322–23 (3.16), 350–51 (3.20), 452, note 3.

154   *try*: "refine, purify by fire; also, remove (the dross or impurity) . . . by fire"; *OED*, *v.* †3. *spec.*

160   *The sparkles of the morninge*: stars reflecting the light of the sun (rather than the meteorological phenomena of that name; q.v. Heninger, *Handbook*, 91–93).

164–65   *lusting . . . Adultery*: An anthropomorphic variant on the astrological term "aspects" (from Latin "aspicere:" "to look at"); cf. line 122. Venus shines with benign aspect upon Mars, thus tempering his malignity and stimulating the tendency to love.

166   *allay*: dilution, abatement, tempering; *OED*, *sb.*[1] II.7–8.

168–69   *fire . . . feare*: comets so high in the firmament that they are invisible to all but an "artist"—scientist (*OED*, I.2), or astrologer (*OED*, I.3.b)—through their optical equipment.

169   *Artists*: The artist gestured toward here is surely Thomas Harriot, the first scientist to use the telescope to assist in astronomical observations (in doing so he anticipated even Galileo, Milton's "*Tuscan* Artist"); John W. Shirley, *Thomas Harriot: A Biography* (Oxford: Clarendon Press, 1983), 397–98. Harriot claimed to have observed nine comets, and to have predicted seven of them—a claim that suggests he saw (or thought he saw) many comets of which his contemporaries were ignorant; John Aubrey, *Brief Lives, chiefly of Contemporaries, set down by John Aubrey, between the Years 1669 & 1696*, ed. Andrew Clark, 2 vols. (Oxford, 1898), 1:285. Harriot certainly observed those of 1607 and 1618, on which he made careful notes; Shirley, *Harriot*, 393–97, 416–17. His use of the "perspective" to observe comets was widely known among English intellectuals, and he was regarded as an authority on them: see Richard Corbett's verse epistle to Thomas Aylesbury on the occasion of the 1618 comet; *The Poems of Richard Corbett*, ed. J. A. W. Bennett and H. R. Trevor-Roper (Oxford: Clarendon Press, 1955), 63–65, 135–38. The poet's denial that the comet would excite the people's fear was tactful: King James had attempted to allay public anxieties over the portentousness of the 1618 comet by announcing that it was "nothing else but Venus with a fire-brand in her arse," and

Figure 8 Prometheus raising man from a rock; from Ovid,
Metamorphoseos Vulgare (1522). Reproduced by permission of the
Folger Shakespeare Library.

by writing a poem instructing his subjects not to interpret
it as an evil omen; *The Poems of James VI. of Scotland,* ed.
James Craigie, 2 vols., Scottish Text Society, 3d series, 22
and 26 (Edinburgh, 1955 and 1958), 2:172–73, 255–57. Unfortunately, the suggestion that it presaged the death of a monarch appeared to be correct: the queen died within a few months
of its appearance; Chamberlain, 2:185; *Poems of Richard
Corbett,* 67.

170   *Higher then Aire hath place*: above the region of the air: the
region immediately above the earth in the Ptolemaic universe.
The phrase apparently registers a commitment to the new astronomical view that comets are celestial rather than terrestrial in origin. According to the traditional view, comets were
exhalations of earth that combusted in the upper reaches of
the air, or possibly in the lowest reaches of the fiery region
beyond (Aristotle, *Meteorologica,* 344a–345a; Heninger, *Handbook,* 87–91). The question of what they might otherwise be

Figure 9 Inigo Jones, Torchbearer; from *The Lords' Masque* (1613).
Reproduced by permission of the Chatsworth Settlement Trustees.

was one of the major astronomical debates of the age, in which interest was especially marked in the wake of the comet of 1618; Lynn Thorndike, *A History of Magic and Experimental Science*, vols. 5–6: *The Sixteenth Century* (New York: Columbia University Press, 1941), chapter 23 (6:67–98); Galileo Galilei, et al., *The Controversy on the Comets of 1618*, trans. Stillman Drake and C. D. O'Malley (Philadelphia: University of Pennsylvania Press, 1960); *Poems of Richard Corbett*, 65; Shirley, *Harriot*, 417.

171   *thunderbolts amazinge flight*: Thunderbolts (lightning bolts, flashing towards earth) were thought to be generated in the cold, moist middle region of air, being caused by earthly exhalations or falling stars cooling there; Aristotle, *Meteorologica*, 342a, 371a; Heninger, *Handbook*, 73–74.

172   *starres coole shootinge*: Shooting, or falling, stars were thought to be caused by earthly exhalations condensing in the moist lower air and dropping back to earth; they thus differed from comets, which were generated in the upper region of air; Aristotle, *Meteorologica*, 342a; Heninger, *Handbook*, 96–97.

173   *sparkes of Junoes Jealousy*: meteors of the airy region, governed by Juno; Heninger, *Handbook*, 45–46.

175   *Deale*: deliver or give; *OED, v.* I.5.

181–82   *Recov'ringe . . . judgment*: Prometheus, a Titan (according to Hesiod's *Theogony*), here sees himself as a descendant of the Giants. This may be due either to the common Renaissance confusion of Titans and Giants, or to the notion that both races were born of Earth.

185   *weare*: spend or pass its time; *OED, v.* V.18.a.

186   *glaunce*: glance (obsolete form of); *OED*.

188   *attempt*: assault, attack; *OED*.

188   *daunger*: damage, endanger (obsolete verb form); *OED*.

192   *Calmely looke . . . desire*: The calm, orderly gaze of the audience is distinguished, Platonically, from the frenzied,

unregulated passion of the Giants: see *Republic*, 403a–b; *Phaedrus*, 237–38.

193   *Ad to the fire*: A notion deriving from Plato's assertion that the fire within is a part of the universal fire, to which we may add; *Philebus*, 29b–d.

199–205   *To close . . . thence*: cf. Jonson, *Love Restored* (1612), lines 214–17.

206   *The discovery of the maine maske*: Presumably a *tableau vivant* featuring those who had danced the antimasque of Giants now dressed as the Nine Worthies, on the conventional attributes of which, see figures 10–11. Cf. Middleton, *The Inner Temple Masque, or Masque of Heroes* (1619), lines 322–24 (ed. R. C. Bald, in T. J. B. Spencer and Stanley Wells, gen. eds., *A Book of Masques: In Honour of Allardyce Nicoll* [Cambridge: Cambridge University Press, 1967], 267); Middleton and Rowley, *A Courtly Masque*, lines 250–99 (*The Works of Thomas Middleton*, ed. A. H. Bullen, 8 vols. [London, 1885–86], 7:164–66).

208   *spring*: "A springing up, growing, or bursting forth of plants, vegetation, etc.; . . . also, a race or stock of persons"; *OED*, sb.[1] III.11.

209   *one*: own (obsolete form of); *OED*.

209   *your one sun*: love: a fire in the heart expressed through the eyes. A Platonic figure: the eye receives fire and light from the sun (intramission), which it then transmits in a sun-like manner (extramission), illuminating that on which it gazes; Plato, *Republic*, 6.507d–509; *Timaeus*, 45b–d; cf. Plotinus, *Enneads*, 1.6.9; Leone Ebreo, *The Philosophy of Love (Dialoghi d'Amore)*, trans. F. Friedberg-Seeley and Jean H. Barnes (London: Soncino, 1937), 212–15. That love was expressed through the eyes was a commonplace: see Ficino, *De Amore*, 7.4, 10.

217   *Let . . . move*: cf. Jonson, "A Celebration of Charis in ten Lyrick Peeces," "I. His Excuse for loving": "Let it not your wonder move" (line 1).

Figure 10 **Godfrey of Bulloigne**; from Thomas Trevelyon's Commonplace Book (1608), fol. 146r. Reproduced by permission of the Folger Shakespeare Library.

Figure 11 Inigo Jones, Statue for the Palace of Perfection (?).
Reproduced by permission of the Chatsworth Settlement Trustees.

217   *wonder*: lady, dancing partner: in the sense of "something
            that causes astonishment"; *OED, sb.* I.

221–22   *Must . . . harmony*: cf. Jonson, *Love Restored:* "Till all be-
            come one *harmonie*" (line 263).

233   *Fillinge each place*: cf. Jonson, *News from the New World*
            (1620): "*But with your motions fill the place*" (line 323).

234   *Where musicke threatens vacancy*: cf. Campion, *The Lords'*
            Masque: "while we with musicke | Fill the emptie space"
            (258).

Studies

ONE

Diplomatic and Literary Contexts

The French Embassy of 1621

On Monday, 8 January 1621, a party of visiting French courtiers and diplomats spent an agreeable day watching Prince Charles and several young English nobles at tilt.[1] While this display of martial prowess and skill in equitation may not have impressed them—the French, as everyone knew, led the world in horsemanship—the sight of eight English courtiers jolting, sweating, and bashing one another with lances must have elicited in the visitors a pleasant feeling of *sang froid*, for their embassy had not been running smoothly.

The French embassy, under the vain and haughty maréchal de Cadenet (brother to the French royal favorite, the duc de Luynes), had arrived in England a fortnight earlier, and little since their arrival had gone to according to plan.[2] Cadenet had been dispatched, as ambassador extraordinary, to convey to King James the fraternal greetings of Louis XIII, who had recently visited Calais. He set out with an enormous entourage of 52 nobles and over 300 followers.[3] On arrival at Dover he was outraged to find that his embassy—which included the crème de la crème of the French nobility—was not being treated with due dignity: nobody was there to meet him, and no adequate accommodations had been prepared. By the time Lord Arundel greeted him at Gravesend he was in high dudgeon. He snubbed Arundel, declining to escort him out of his chambers; and Arundel (unwilling to take the insult) snubbed him back, insisting on meeting him the next day in the street.[4]

While Cadenet had reason to feel aggrieved about this chaotic reception, it was the result, not of sinister diplomatic maneuvering, but of poor communication and incompetence. The English had only heard of the impending visit around 13 December, and they only knew of Cadenet's imminent arrival a few days later (by 22 December).[5] The king was then in the country, hunting at his beloved Theobalds, where he had planned to spend Christmas—in part no doubt to avoid having to pay for the festivities of a court season in a period of financial embarrassment.[6] Cadenet's reception was bodged together at the last minute: there were bound to be hitches.

The King's Chamber Accounts for the period show various craftsmen being employed to prepare accommodations and other necessaries for Cadenet and his train. John Gosnold, a gentleman usher, was charged with appareling "Denmark House" (Somerset House) for the Ambassador's lodgings, and Inigo Jones, as Surveyor of the King's Works, made certain special arrangements there.[7] John Hebborne, another gentleman usher, spent several days working with eight assistants to prepare hangings and furniture in Whitehall for the royal family (his work included the readying of a room for Prince Charles to rehearse his masque). Hebborne also prepared Parliament House for the reception of Cadenet and his embassy, and Essex House "for feasting him."[8]

Despite all this activity, matters hardly improved after Cadenet's arrival in London. On hearing of the ambassador's conduct towards Arundel, the king flew into a fury. An audience was arranged for the ambassador in Westminster: the king came down the river from Whitehall by barge, and the ambassador made his way up the Strand from "Denmark House" by coach. The audience must have been a moderate success, for a second was granted that evening—a private audience, at which only he and the marquess of Buckingham were present. It lasted two hours.[9] Apart from this show of royal approval, things were not going entirely to the satisfaction of either host or visitors. On 4 January another public audience was scheduled, on which Cadenet and his entourage were to dine with the king and court in Westminster Hall: it was an enormous feast, the like of which had not been seen—so the ballad makers claimed—since the time of King Stephen.[10] To accommodate the party, the fixed seating had been ripped out of the hall.[11] Despite all efforts, however, there had to be an overflow; a second feast was laid out in the Court of Requests. With extraordinary temerity, Cadenet kept the king cooling his heels for over an hour—the antipaste ready on the tables— before sauntering in to dine. Those members of his party who were led to dine in the Court of Requests felt slighted. When Chancellor Bacon and his colleagues arrived and sat down unceremoniously in their gowns it was the last straw: several Frenchmen left the room, grumbling at the indignity of being forced to dine with these "*Messieurs de robe longue.*" Poor Sir John Finett—the royal master of ceremonies, whose job it was to see to the comfort of the visitors—was a very busy man.[12]

But the entertainment continued: that afternoon there was a ball at Whitehall and, on the following day, running at the ring. On Twelfth Night, Prince Charles presented his masque at Whitehall before the ambassador and the more important of his embassy: this was, we have recently been shown, *Pan's Anniversary*, with a text by Ben Jonson and scenes by Inigo Jones.[13] And now, two days later, after a hard day's tilting, there was to be another feast and another masque—an entertainment, in fact, to crown all the others. It

was anticipated with excitement, for its host was not the uncouth and impoverished monarch, but Viscount Doncaster,
the most munificent man and the most accomplished courtier
in Britain; a man who, as the ballad makers put it, excelled in
"French compliments."[14]

Viscount Doncaster and his Magnificent Entertainments

James Hay, Viscount Doncaster, and later first earl of Carlisle, was a Scot who had accompanied King James to London
and had, like several of his countrymen, gained enormous sums
of money on account of his appeal to the king. Though never
uniquely in the royal favor, he was nonetheless seldom out of
it.[15] Unusually for a royal favorite (one of those courtiers sin-
gled out by the king for peculiar attention), he did not possess
a particularly handsome profile ("Thou ugly, filthy, camel's
face," Princess Elizabeth used to address him—not without
justification: see figure 12).[16] Doncaster's hold over the king
lay in his gracious demeanor and personal charm. He was,
according to Arthur Wilson, "A true Courtier for complying,
and one that had Language enough to be *real* as well as *formal*; for he could personate both to the height of *expression*."[17]
As Wilson implies, there was substance beneath the surface.
Despite his posthumous reputation as a fatuous profligate,
he was a skilled diplomat and a canny politician with foreign
and domestic agendas of his own. Prime among these was a
belief in the need for a European Protestant alliance to offset
the dominance of the combined Habsburg and Papal forces—
a belief that led him, for the greater part of his career, to push
for a French dynastic marriage.[18] Such views allied him firmly
with the anti-Spanish or "puritan" faction in the early 1620s.[19]
Although he had been forced to back away temporarily from
the public urging of the interests of the deposed Palatine

Figure 12   James Hay, Viscount Doncaster, first earl of Carlisle
(c. 1628). Reproduced by courtesy of the National Portrait Gallery,
London.

Elector, Frederick and his wife, Elizabeth (King James's daughter), in the wake of Spanish complaints that he had been warmongering during his peacemaking mission of 1619, he remained a firm supporter both of the hapless couple and of the European Protestant cause.[20] As maréchal de Bassompierre noted during his English embassy of 1626, Doncaster was a tricky customer, "qui est fort Puritain, & qui fait le subtil dans ca religion."[21]

Doncaster was unique among Jacobean courtiers in his mastery of the French *manière*. Like a number of his countrymen he had, as a youth, been educated in France, where he imbibed the skills and accomplishments of the French courtier. He owed his first presentation to James to his patron, Charles Cauchon de Maupas, baron le Tour, the French ambassador in Scotland, and he did not forget his debt: he remained for many years a committed Francophile, a firm supporter of French interests and a French alliance.[22] His understanding of French mores was widely noticed—the painter Rubens, meeting him in the later 1620s, remarked upon it; and it led him to be dispatched on several important diplomatic missions to Paris.[23] The most recent was that of 1616, on the eve of which he had ordered his entire wardrobe to be retailored, at enormous expense, having heard, at the eleventh hour, of a change in Parisian fashions. On his arrival, he made a great impression by riding a horse shod with silver shoes—shoes attached loosely enough to fly off into the crowd at regular intervals.[24] All in all, he handled the ceremonial aspects of his embassy with such elan that even the Spanish were put to shame by his magnificence.[25]

At the court of King James, wrote Arthur Wilson, "All the study was, who should be most glorious, and he had the happiest *fancy*, whose invention could express something *Novel*, neat, and unusual, that others might admire."[26] In the relentless quest for novelty and glory, Hay gave place to no one. He established a reputation for extravagance that was unparalleled even at this most prodigal of courts. "He was surely," wrote Clarendon in later years, "a man of the greatest expense in his own person of any in the age he lived, and introduced more of that expense in the excess of clothes and diet than any other man; and was indeed the original of all those inventions from which others did but transcribe copies."[27] The schedule of Doncaster's debts preserved in the House of Lords Record Office confirms the aptness of Clarendon's remark.[28] Doncaster's clothing exerted a peculiar fascination upon his contemporaries. Wilson recalled seeing him clad in one of his meaner outfits:

> the Cloak and Hose were made of very fine white Beaver, imbroidered richly all over with Gold and Silver; the Cloak, almost to the Cape, within and without, having no lining but imbroidery, The Doublet was Cloth of Gold, imbroidered so thick, that it could not be discerned, and a white Beaver-hat suitable, Brimfull of imbroidery, both above and below[29]

While Wilson did not hold Doncaster solely responsible for the Jacobean obsession with gorgeous apparel, he did attribute to him the introduction of lavish feasting and banqueting, and associated this with his reception in France in 1616 where, according to John Chamberlain, he was entertained with several feasts, a number of which cost in the region of £1000.[30] It may have been from France that Doncaster drew the inspiration for the most notorious invention attributed to him—the antesupper:

> The manner of which was, to have the board covered, at the first entrance of the Ghests, with dishes, as high as a tall man could well reach, filled with the choycest and dearest viands sea or land could afford: And all this once seene and having feasted the eyes of the Invited, was in a manner throwne away, and fresh set on to the same height, having only this advantage of the other, that it was hot.[31]

Whether or not the antesupper ever actually took place in precisely this fashion (and the solitary testimony of Francis Osborne's retrospective and highly moralized account makes one a little suspicious), the attribution reveals much about contemporary estimates of Hay's character and taste.[32] In light of such extravagance, we may understand the glee with which contemporaries recorded the aptness of Hay's eventual demise from a consumption.[33] Such enormous expense and conspicuous consumption was not, of course, pointless prodigality; it was a public demonstration of the magnificence of the courtier and the munificence of the monarch. By employing the gifts of royal largesse in a conspicuous manner on clothes and feasts, rather than investing it for his own benefit in land or stock, Hay offered an immediate and visible return of glory to the king. This was a view expressed in his *impresa* for a tournament of 1610: a circle adorned with the motto, "Redit, unde fuit"—"It returns whence it came."[34]

Although best remembered for his sartorial and culinary innovations, Hay was also a generous and discerning sponsor of the arts. He might not have been able to compete with Lord Arundel, his near neighbour, as a connoisseur of the visual arts, but he nonetheless took more than a passing interest in the collection of hangings and paintings.[35] His gift to Charles I of a painting bequeathed him to by John Donne affords a glimpse into the circulation of works of art in his milieu.[36] Donne was only one of many men of letters who entered Doncaster's orbit and received his support.[37] Doncaster attracted laudatory poems or dedications from such literary figures as Joshua Sylvester, John Davies of Hereford, John Ford, Nicholas Oldisworth, the German poet Georg Rudolf Weckherlin, and members of a circle of Scottish poets who made their approaches to him in the early years of James's reign—a group that included Sir Robert Ayton, Alexander Craig, Arthur Johnston, and John Leech.[38] But it was not poetry that interested Doncaster so much as music and the masque. He adored vocal music, and was known to weep at a moving lute song.[39] He kept a number of household musicians whom he employed in entertainments: their presentation of a song to the earl of Salisbury at Newmarket in October 1632 is noted in the account books of that earl.[40] An avid masquer in his youth, Doncaster had danced in *Hymenaei* (1606), *The Haddington Masque* (1608), *The Lords' Masque* (1613), and *The Somerset Masque* (1613).[41] In later years, when he was no longer young and agile enough to dance, he continued to take part in private theatricals and encouraged his family to dance in masques, scoffing at his son's complaints about uncomfortable costumes.[42] During the latter years of James's reign he turned to sponsorship.

Doncaster's masques invariably fell within the compass of a full evening's entertainment, and they should probably be read with some awareness of that context. Their conventional placement between the void (a ceremonial serving of wines and spices while the tables were cleared) and the banquet (a light course of costly and elaborately decorated sweetmeats) dictated their length and the circumstances of their reception.[43] In February 1617 *Lovers Made Men*, a masque written by Jonson and designed by Nicholas Lanier, was performed at his official residence at the Wardrobe in Blackfriars for his old patron, the French ambassador, baron le Tour.[44] The evening featured both a feast and a masque. The masque was hailed by one observer as the equal of those seen at Whitehall, and the feast as "the most magnificent feast thatt ever I have seene in my life"; another commentator noted that the feast was "the most sumptuous that hath bene seen here for many yeares."[45] It cost over £2200 and featured "seven score fesants, twelve partridges in a dish throughout, twelve whole samons, and whatsoever els that cost or curiositie could procure in like superfluitie: besides the workemanship and inventions of

thirtie cookes for twelve dayes."[46] The success of this occasion may have prompted Doncaster's decision to offer another
masque on New Year's Day 1618: *The Masque of Amazons,
or The Ladies Masque*, which was to have been presented to
the royal couple by his wife, in the role of queen of the Amazons. This masque, however, met with royal disapproval ("neither the Quene nor King did like or allow of yt") and was
cancelled.[47] While the queen may have felt irritated by the
usurpation by Doncaster's wife of a role she herself had played
a decade before in the *Masque of Queens*, the king's disapproval probably focused on its militaristic theme, stridently
at odds with the royal pacifism—a suggestion given weight by
the involvement in the masque of a number of women from
the aggressively pro-Protestant Sidney and Rich families.[48] The
cancellation of *The Masque of Amazons* was sufficiently dis-
couraging to dissuade Doncaster from involving himself in
masquing for some time. Not until January 1620 did he again
host a masque, and that was a safer proposition: he presented
to his wife, at Buckingham's request, the so-called "running
masque," an established success, entertaining its audience and
participants "in the most lavish and splendid manner."[49]

In addition to *Lovers Made Men*, texts for several masques
in which Doncaster was involved survive. *Lord Hay's Masque*,
written by Thomas Campion and designed by Inigo Jones for
Hay's nuptials, was performed at court at the expense of his
family and friends in January 1607.[50] Hay was, in addition,
involved in planning the wedding festivities for Princess Elizabeth in 1613, at which Campion and Jones's *The Lords' Masque*
was performed: he was one of the principal organizers of the
masque, and may have pushed for Campion to be given the
commission for it.[51]

While the character of his involvement differed from masque
to masque, there are some striking points of thematic and
structural similarity between these surviving texts. Like many
masques of the period, all three were concerned with the

lawful conduct of love, and in all three the main masque is structurally and thematically integral to the performance.[52] These are not in themselves distinctive features (particularly since two of them were wedding masques), but the nature of their intersection is noteworthy. Both *Lord Hay's Masque* and *Lovers Made Men* turn upon a divinely inspired transformation in which a group of central figures is retransformed from a state of depravity occasioned by a lust-driven metamorphosis to the assumption of a fully human or divine existence. In the former, nine knights of Apollo, transformed into trees by Cynthia for their sins against chastity, recover their identities through the grace of Apollo; in the latter, ghostly lovers are restored to life. In *The Lords' Masque* the transgression is of a different kind, but a transformation is still involved: eight women, transformed into statues by Jove out of anger at Prometheus's illicit creation of them, are restored to life and paired off with eight animated star-men. Such transformations form the pivot of each masque, and scenic transformations are subordinated to them. *Lord Hay's Masque* featured, at the moment of metamorphosis, the splitting open and disappearance of a grove of trees which concealed the masquers (the trees were moved by a machine hidden beneath a raised stage, down into which they were drawn).[53] A similar effect was achieved without machinery in *Lovers Made Men*, in which a fixed grove of myrtles served to shield the masquers from the audience as they changed their costumes.[54]

The idea of metamorphosis is, of course, central to the masque; but it is generally associated with scenic change, and rarely features as a structural principle involving the transformation of antimasquers to masquers. The blanching of the daughters of Niger takes place in the three year gap separating the *Masque of Blackness* (1605) from the *Masque of Beauty* (1608); but here, as Stephen Orgel points out, the transformation is implied rather than represented.[55] In *The Irish Masque at Court* (1613) Irish ambassadors were anglicized through the benign royal gaze—signified by the removal their *"Irish mantles"*; but such figures were not properly antimasquers, being—though Irish—civilized gentlemen all along (they danced their entry not to some wild skirl but *"to a solemne musique of harpes"*; line 141). *The Golden Age Restored* (1616), by contrast, featured a metamorphosis of rebels to stones—a transformation accompanied by a scene change (lines 66–83). But there is no suggestion in this case that the petrified antimasquers subsequently took part in the main masque. And this, in the end, is what distinguishes the masques involving Hay: the use of metamorphosis as a means of turning the antimasquers into masquers—a device that either permits or is designed to allow for the doubling-up of parts. It appears to have originated in three works with which Doncaster was closely connected. We find its origins in the animated trees of *Lord Hay's Masque* and meet it once again in the statues of *The Lords' Masque*; though in neither of these cases are we dealing with antimasquers strictly defined. The device reaches fruition in *Lovers Made Men*. Other instances of the same conceit, perhaps influenced by Doncaster, may be found in several slightly later works—in *The Gypsies Metamorphosed* (1621), and in the masque recently discovered by James Knowles dating from the period 1619–21.[56]

The masques with which Doncaster was involved are remarkable not only for their use of the antimasquers to perform the masque; they are also distinctive for their use of an unusually small number of performers. *Lord Hay's Masque* featured nine masquers and four named speakers; the text of *Lovers Made Men* mentions six masquers and no more than eleven performers in all.[57] *The Lords' Masque* is more typical in employing eight men, eight women, and four speaking parts. In the case of *Lovers Made Men*, the unusually low number of performers and the doubling-up of parts might be attributed to the limited space available in the Wardrobe. If restricted space was in fact the initial motive for the doubling-up, Jonson nonetheless managed to manufacture a fable that would make the best use of the unusual presence of the same figures in both antimasque and masque.[58] And restrictions on space will not explain the doubling-up of parts in *Lord Hay's Masque*, which was presented at Whitehall. Here an aesthetic decision was made, and we would be rash to dismiss too readily the implications of Campion's justification of the appearance of precisely nine masquers:

> *Their number Nine, the best and amplest of numbers, for as in Musicke seven notes containe all varietie, the eight being in nature the same with the first, so in numbring after the ninth we begin again, the tenth beeing as it were the Diappason in Arithmetick. The number of 9 is famed by the Muses and Worthies, and it is of all the most apt for chaunge and diversitie of proportion.*[59]

Campion's numerological organization of the masque extended even to the proportions of the stage and the number of musicians employed in the performance.[60] Such thinking seems to have struck a chord in the Doncaster household. The cancelled *Masque of Amazons* was to have featured nine ladies, including Hay's wife.[61] Doncaster's interest in doing things by threes and nines appears to have been common knowledge at court. On the eve of his departure on his French embassy of 1616, Lady Haddington quipped that "the flowre and bewtie of his embassage consists in three mignards [*i.e. minions*], three daunsers, and three fooles or buffons."[62]

The similarities between the several masques in which Doncaster was closely involved may in part be explained by reference to continuities in their personnel: Campion and Jones produced both *Lord Hay's Masque* and *The Lords' Masque*, while Jonson and Lanier produced *Lovers Made Men*. The only constant between all three masques is, however, Doncaster

himself; and the distinctive structural feature they share—
the transformation of antimasquers into masquers—is best
explained by reference to Doncaster's taste—a taste shaped
by his early exposure to the French *ballet de cour*, and confirmed by his entertainment with *ballets* and other "diver-
tissements" on his embassy of 1616.[63] Enid Welsford has drawn
attention to a number of possible connections between
French *ballets* and English masques, and John Peacock has
detected French influences in the Jacobean designs of Inigo
Jones.[64] It is nonetheless fair to say that, with the exception
of the highly influential *Balet Comique* of Balthasar Beaujoyeulx (1581), we lack a clear sense of the extent of French
influence on the texts of masques prior to Charles's marriage
to Henrietta Maria.[65] The matter may be clarified by recog-
nizing Doncaster's importance as an impetus for French influence on the English masque prior to the French marriage.[66]
He was a generous sponsor of French poets and musicians. On
his embassy to Paris in 1616 he appears to have been con-
tacted by the court poet Marc de Mailliet, who addressed a
poem to him.[67] Soon afterwards, de Mailliet visited England
and penned a *ballet* for Queen Anne: we are probably right to
see Doncaster's hand at work in this commission.[68]

The printed text of the *Balet de la revanche du mespris
d'Amour* (London, 1617) shows it to have possessed the characteristic inconsequence of the French *ballets*.[69] It featured a
series of more or less arbitrary entries by lovers of various
sorts—faithful, rebellious, ridiculous—who were presented by
Cupid to the queen. James Knowles suggests that this was the
ballet performed by the queen's French musicians at Somerset House on 19 February 1617, and that it therefore provided
a fable to which Jonson responded three nights later in *Lovers
Made Men*.[70] Be that as it may, it was evidently a novel entertainment to the English, who left its production to French
musicians and its performance to a visiting troupe of French
dancers (Inigo Jones, however, appears to have designed it).[71]

Those who saw it were not quite sure what to make of it: John Chamberlain described it as "a kind of maske or antique."[72] While this performance may not have met with great success, Hay continued to take an active interest in French poetry and French styles of entertainment. On his embassy of 1623 he held an audience with the poet Malherbe, and in 1625 he presented an ode by the dramatist and poet Boisrobert to Henrietta Maria.[73] French musicians also enjoyed his patronage. He employed Nicholas Lanier to produce the music for *Lovers Made Men*, and he was connected with the lutenist (and murderer) Jacques Gaultier, who, under interrogation in the late 1620s for suspected complicity in a plot to assassinate Buckingham, claimed to have conducted an illicit liaison with Doncaster's daughter.[74]

French influence may be detected in several aspects of the masques in which Doncaster was closely involved. Enid Welsford long ago attributed the doubling-up of masquers as antimasquers in *Lovers Made Men* to the model of the French *ballets*, in which dancers often made several different appearances.[75] And she proposed that the invention of *Lord Hay's Masque*, with its retransformation of trees back into knights, may have been suggested by a French *mascarade* of 1565 by Jean Antoine de Baïf, in which knights and ladies turned into rocks and trees are reanimated by the power of Amphion.[76] Metamorphosis was, in fact, one of the staple features of the French *ballet de cour*.[77] A strongly French flavor has also been detected in Lanier's early English employment of recitative singing in *Lovers Made Men*, an innovation apparently designed to compliment the visiting French ambassador.[78] We might add that both Campion's and Jonson's texts for Doncaster are close in theme and fable to several recent French *ballets*, a number of which—*Le Ballet des Argonautes* (1614) and *La Délivrance de Persée* (1617), in particular—dealt with the problem of passion and featured the metamorphoses of their performers.[79] It might even be that the unperformed

Masque of Amazons—a vehicle for Doncaster's wife—was based upon the French *Ballet des Amazons* of 1608.[80]

All this helps us to imagine that Cadenet and his party may have been in unusually good spirits as they made their way down the Strand to Essex House, Doncaster's riverside accommodation, on the evening of 8 January (figure 13).[81] It does not, however, explain what they were doing in England in the first place.

Foreign and Domestic Affairs in 1620–21

Repeated audiences and secret meetings are not really consonant with the routine conveyance of fraternal greetings between monarchs. The true purpose of the embassy—and one of which contemporaries were well aware—was more complex and diplomatically sensitive. Europe teetered on the brink of a catastrophic war.[82] Divided by two major alliances—the Catholic League (with power-bases in Spain, Italy, and Austria) and the Protestant Union (a loose coalition of German states and principalities)—Europe had been in a state of uneasy tension for many years, with France and England holding the balance. James wished to keep this balance in his hands, playing the role of mediator. Having married his daughter Elizabeth to Frederick, the Elector Palatine, who headed the Protestant Union, he was now pushing for a Spanish marriage for his son. It was an elegant plan; but James was not a lucky monarch. Things began to go wrong when, in 1618, the Bohemians ejected their Catholic king, and invited the Elector Frederick to take the crown. Against James's advice, he did so. In the meantime, the deposed king, Ferdinand, had been elected Holy Roman Emperor, and had acquired, as a consequence, some very powerful friends. These included his relatives in Spain, who were then intent upon regaining their grasp upon the Netherlands—an assault for which they required

Figure 13 Essex House (far right) and environs, from Wenceslaus Hollar, "Bird's-eye View of London" (c. 1646). Reproduced by permission of the British Museum.

a secure route through Germany. The Habsburgs marshaled their forces in middle Europe, routing Frederick in November 1620 at the Battle of the White Mountain. The Elector and his wife fled, only to find that their hereditary lands in the Palatinate had, in their absence, been occupied by Habsburg forces, intent upon securing the Rhine. This was too much for King James to ignore: he might tolerate Frederick's expulsion from Bohemia, to which he had no legitimate claim; but the Palatinate was his by right. He thus demanded that the Palatinate be restored. In this, France saw her opportunity.

The recent military and diplomatic successes of the Catholic League were a grave worry to France, who looked increasingly vulnerable, surrounded, as she was, by Habsburg territories. If she were to prevent Habsburg control of the disputed territory of the Valteline (an alpine region which gave Spanish forces in Italy a backdoor into France) and guarantee her continued viability as an independent force, France needed at the very least to disrupt the move towards an Anglo-Spanish alliance (a growing possibility given the advanced stage of the marriage negotiations and the rising influence of the Spanish ambassador, Gondomar, at the English court). Better still would be an Anglo-French alliance cemented upon a dynastic marriage—although any such suggestion would need to be broached with the greatest tact, given Spanish priority in the matter. The current inclination of the English people and, it appeared, her monarch, toward a Protestant offensive to recover the Palatinate made this a propitious time for such a proposal, for England would, in such an undertaking, be foolish to ignore the offer of French support.

Foreign policy was not, however, the only issue for the embassy. French domestic stability was threatened by the activities of an illegal assembly of Huguenot leaders at La Rochelle: a civil war seemed imminent. Protestant England must therefore be dissuaded from intervening on behalf of her coreligionists. While James's pacifism and his well-known financial difficulties made any such intervention unlikely, if not impossible, his issue on 6 November of a proclamation summoning a Parliament early in the new year suddenly changed the whole picture. Parliament was summoned for the clear purpose of raising money to support a bid to recover the Palatinate (although James hoped that the mere threat of such a Parliament would allow him to settle the dispute peacefully). Many of its members would be seriously committed to a pan-European Protestant offensive.[83]

Cadenet's embassy had, therefore, two major aims: to stall the rise of Habsburg influence (broaching, if possible, the idea of a marriage between Prince Charles and Henrietta Maria), and to gain a guarantee that England would not intervene in the Huguenot affair. He set out to do so by casting the problem in political rather than religious terms, portraying the Huguenot problem as a purely civil dispute. This was a strategy admirably designed to appeal to James's jealous guarding of the royal prerogative; and it was buttressed by the prospect of a French marriage and military support for the Elector.[84] But the communication of such objectives was a task that required a delicate touch, and Cadenet was precisely the wrong man to perform it.

For the English king, the French embassy provided an opportunity for some elaborate diplomatic maneuvering. James wished to use it to dissuade the French from using force against the Huguenots, implying that he might intervene on their behalf (something he had in fact neither the will nor the means to accomplish); and he wanted to frighten the Habsburgs into rapid conciliation over the Palatinate and agreement upon a Spanish marriage for Prince Charles by feigning an interest in the French proposal. For James, therefore, the entertainment of the French ambassador was primarily an exercise in dissimulation and disinformation—an exercise for which he happily exploited Doncaster and others.[85] Thus James met with Cadenet and listened to the ambassador's critique of the Huguenots, while refusing to acknowledge the validity of his distinction between toleration for their religious principles and the need to respond to their political disobedience.[86] But behind the ambassador's back James met in secret with a Huguenot who had accompanied the embassy, using Doncaster's house in which to do so.[87] By negotiating with the French through Doncaster and the Secretary of State, Robert Naunton—two well-known advocates of a French alliance— the king protected himself and his favorite, Buckingham, from Spanish anger, should his elaborate scheme fall apart—as of course it did.[88]

The Bohemian problem was not, however, a purely foreign affair; it had frightening repercussions at home. Although James understood that the next step after the Protestant marriage of his daughter was a Catholic match for his son, many of his subjects had different views. What they wanted was a resumption of the old, Elizabethan foreign policy: staunchly Protestant and aggressively anti-Habsburg. They saw the Protestant match as a step in this direction, and they interpreted James's current attempts to arrange Spanish marriage as a sign that he had lost his way, a sign that he was being misled by corrupt advisors who wished to undo the reformation and betray England into the hands of Spain and the Pope. Frederick's decision to accept the crown of Bohemia was thus a critical moment for this so-called "puritan" faction: they expected an immediate show of support, and expressed their views in an explosion of public discussion, letter-writing, pamphleteering, and versifying, the like of which had never been seen.[89] After the summoning of Parliament in early November and the catastrophe at the White Mountain later that month, such discussion grew deafening.

To a monarch as jealous of his prerogative as James, the mere discussion of matters of state by his subjects was an affront to his authority; the criticism of his foreign policy implied by the current discussion was intolerable. With a Parliament in the offing—a Parliament that would contain many vocal supporters of the Bohemian cause—the threat of serious meddling in foreign policy loomed large. To silence such discourse, and to remind his subjects (and his new MPs) of their own limited grasp of such matters, he ordered Chancellor Bacon to draft a stern *Proclamation against excesse of Lavish and Licentious Speech of matters of State*. The proclamation warned James's subjects against the discussion of "matters of State, (which are no Theames, or subjects fit for vulgar persons, or common meetings," decrying their "excesse and presumption," and urging them to "containe themselves within that modest and reverent regard, of matters, above their reach and calling." It was issued on 24 December 1620.[90]

It was probably in response to this threat to the royal prerogative that the marquess of Buckingham seized on the idea of a royally endorsed "academy of honor." This scheme was the brainchild of Edmund Bolton (a client and minor Leicestershire kinsman of the marquess), who saw it as a means to prevent the decay of honor (a direct result of James's promiscuous sale of titles), and to combat disobedience to the king—"the encroachments, practises, and importunities of CONFUSION, and BARBAROUSNESSE." What Bolton envisaged was the conversion of Windsor Castle into a bootcamp for minor and new nobility, who would there be instructed in "the doctrines, & exercises of HONOR," in "moral vertue," and in "heroick knowledges" by members of the Order of the Garter. Such instruction would lead these nobles to a clearer understanding of their function as pillars of the royal prerogative, and would, through their example, improve public manners and buttress the power of the crown.[91] A manuscript proposal for the scheme was dedicated and presented to Buckingham in late December 1620 ("before Christmasse"): its painted frontispiece depicts the marquess as St. George, slaughtering the dragon of barbarousness (figure 14). The proposal clearly took hold. A version of it, recommending the establishment of "an Academy, for the directing and bringing up of the Nobility and Gentry of this Kingdom, in their younger and tender Age," was proposed by Buckingham in the House of Lords on 5 March 1621, and a committee, including Doncaster, Arundel, and the first earl of Clare, was set up to report on it.[92]

Such arguments over the Bohemian problem were not restricted to the broadsheet and the royal edict. The argument over the appropriate response to the crisis had been played out in the masques and entertainments of the previous year or so. In April 1619 the Dutch ambassadors had been entertained by the artillery company with "a warlike daunce or maske of twelve men in compleat armor."[93] In their *Courtly Masque: The Device, called The World tost at Tennis*, a work performed some time between the autumn of 1619 and the summer of 1620, Thomas Middleton and William Rowley had responded to the crisis with a daringly unambiguous call for action in defense of the Palatinate.[94] Their strange, generic melange (it is part masque, part drama), presents a world corrupted by the courtly vices of pride and deceit, a world in which arms and arts, embodied in the figures of a scholar and a soldier, are impoverished and degenerate, and where "Minerva's altars all are ruin'd now" (line 209). To indict this fallen world Pallas (embodiment of the ideal combination of arms and arts) and Jupiter introduce a vision of the Nine Worthies—those whom "the young world, I In her unstable youth, did then produce" (lines 252–53), and who were distinguished for their valorous actions, in contrast to the merely contemplative men of the present, who "strive to know too much, too little do" (line 307). The fallen world is then redeemed by a king who reassigns the correct value to each of the professions under his purview, giving due credit to the soldier: the masque ends on a stridently martial note, with the soldier departing to defend the Palatinate—"I'll over yonder, to the most glorious

Figure 14 Marquess of Buckingham as St. George (1620), by
Edmund Bolton; BL, Harleian MS 6103, fol. 3r. Reproduced by
permission of the British Library.

wars | That e'er fam'd Christian kingdom" (lines 877–78)—
and Prince Charles himself, rather improbably, preparing to
don his armor (lines 863–65).[95] The decay of the world and
Pallas's restoration of order are tropes that had earlier appeared
in Jonson's *Golden Age Restored* (1616)—a masque to which
Middleton and Rowley may well have been indebted. Unlike
Jonson's masque, however, the *Courtly Masque* was never
actually performed at court; for it could not have been further
removed from the king's pacific response to the Bohemian crisis, or more clearly allied with the strident Protestant militarism he so feared and despised.[96]

   To such astonishingly oppositional texts, Ben Jonson's
masques of the period, stand as orthodox, courtly rebukes.[97]
News from the New World, performed on Twelfth Night
1620, denounced the circulation of news and its implied criticism of the royal foreign policy; and *Pan's Anniversary*, the
masque performed by the prince on Twelfth Night 1621,
shamelessly ingratiated itself with the Spanish party, and with
the two French ambassadors to whom it was presented, in its
attack on those who called for military action in defence of
European Protestantism.[98] Whereas the *Courtly Masque* of
Middleton and Rowley corrects English indolence and irre-
sponsibility with a call for heroic, military action, *Pan's
Anniversary* presents England as a golden world of pastoral
otium rudely invaded by a generically and politically inappropriate militarism.[99] Middleton's heroic vision of Charles
as a new Prince Henry, buckling on his armour in defence of
the Protestant cause, is replaced by Jonson's pastoral vision
of the prince as a shepherd, enjoying the "peace and pleasure"
afforded by "*Great* Pan"; and in one of the metamorphoses that
seem to have been the order of the day, the intruders are transformed into sheep, allowing the shepherds to resume their
rustic revelry (lines 255, 239–40). The seasonal delights of the
court are not for long disrupted by foreign troubles. Small

wonder that those with pan-Protestant sympathies were offended by the masque's introduction of a puritan, "to be flowted and abused."[100]

The problem of social and political order at home; the crisis of Protestantism abroad; and the question of the marriage settlement for the prince: this was the interwoven complex of issues which impinged upon Doncaster's guests as they made their way to Essex House on 8 January 1621.

Two

&

The Masque

Occasion

Doncaster's guests included Cadenet and a select number of his party, the king and Prince Charles, the marquess of Buckingham and his wife, the countesses of Dorset and of Warwick, and "most of the great Lords and Ladies in Towne."[1] In presenting a masque to such a gathering, Doncaster had a peculiarly delicate task, which involved both risks and opportunities; for the masque was not merely presented to the ambassador on behalf of the king, it was also offered to the king by Doncaster: our understanding of the masque depends upon our grasp of its peculiar status and location.

Unlike a masque at Whitehall, offered within the bounds of the royal palace and at the king's expense, this was presented at a private residence by a courtier to his guests. At one level, it was not an official court masque, but a private entertainment for a monarch and select members of the court. As such, it approaches the status occupied by the "running masque" of the previous season, or that of *The Gypsies*

Metamorphosed of the following summer, both of which were presented to the king in several noble households at various removes from the court. Such occasions permitted a degree of informality, license, and irreverence, which Jonson's bawdy and playful gypsies exploited to the full. But the presence of the French ambassador prohibited such freedom and complicated the balance of the entertainment: with the ambassador present, the court was on display here, no less than at Whitehall. And with James present, also, Doncaster's residence became, out of courtesy, the king's. The entertainment could not, therefore, be regarded solely and simply as a private, informal affair; it was also, perforce, an official engagement. The official, or perhaps semiofficial, character of the evening is implied by the fact that the Office of the King's Chamber paid John Hebborne for fitting out Essex House for the feast.[2] The preparation of Doncaster's residence was an official responsibility, even if the furnishing of the feast and the preparation of the masque itself were not. In fact, we cannot know how far royal input dictated the shape of the masque because the Revels Office accounts for this period were never filed.[3]

It was, then, the presence of both ambassador *and* monarch that determined the shape of the event. The presence of the ambassador and the absence of the king would have afforded the poet the freedom to improvise positions that would not necessarily be taken as official policy statements, and the liberty to construct a fiction that did not need to revolve exclusively around the mystique of royalty. In *Lovers Made Men*, the entertainment staged for baron le Tour in 1617, the absence of the king allowed Jonson to concoct an unusually freestanding masque, the action of which is not dependent upon the motivating presence of royalty, and which in consequence approaches the condition of drama.[4] In that masque, the transformation of the lovers is occasioned not by the external agency of royal virtue, but by the power of fate and the agency of Mercury, a character within the fiction itself. This is not to suggest that the masque is in some sense a play, for it still succeeds in breaking down the distinction between fable and reality through the revels, as the reformed lovers take their partners from the audience and dance. Through the judicious selection of an apt fable, Jonson substitutes for the motivating power of monarchy the awful force of love, turning the fiction on the presence in the audience of a number of beautiful and eligible young ladies. Such licence was not available to the inventors of *The Essex House Masque*.

Insofar as it was presented to the ambassador on behalf of the king, the masque had to toe the royal line on the issues that underlay the embassy, and had to do so in a manner at once clear and inoffensive. It therefore needed to avoid offending either the French or the Spanish, who, though excluded from the evening, would surely hear accounts of it. Indeed, given James's desire to use the French embassy to force the Spanish to speed up the marriage negotiations, the absent ambassador Gondomar might legitimately be regarded as its most important auditor. The masque needed to hint at English commitment to recover the Palatinate and at the seriousness of their interest in the French marriage proposal— though it needed to do so without directly addressing such issues, or implicating the king in their expression. As such it needed to depart from the officially endorsed pacifism of *Pan's Anniversary*. Herein lay several opportunities for Doncaster. Insofar as he was seriously committed to both support for Protestantism and a French match, the masque might not only express such initiatives as part of a campaign of royal disinformation, it might also attempt to impress them upon the monarch as serious and desirable options. It might, furthermore, attempt to assuage the king's anxieties about the domestic problems that had attended these international issues—the public discussions, and the threat of the impending Parliament. This was therefore an opportunity for Doncaster to mediate between James and the French, and between the king and his country. Doncaster was too accomplished a courtier to let such an opportunity pass.

Quite aside from such policy questions, Doncaster had some need to demonstrate his continued centrality at court. Over the past few years Buckingham had risen inexorably, consolidating his position through the construction of a network of clients and supporters. Doncaster, who had never operated through faction, was increasingly forced to urge his interests through the now dominant favorite—a humiliating and frequently fruitless endeavor.[5] In league with Arundel, Doncaster was currently showering the new favorite with hospitality, with pictures to educate his taste, and with council to develop his judgement.[6] In January 1620 he had hosted Buckingham's "running masque," and in September, he had entertained Buckingham, his wife, and his mother to "a great feast" at Syon House—the residence of his father-in-law, Henry Percy, ninth earl of Northumberland.[7] The Essex House entertainment gave him a further opportunity to improve and correct the new man's taste. In the previous winter, Doncaster had been imposed upon by Buckingham to host his "running masque"—an entertainment supposedly prepared after the French manner. Remarking on the unusual character of the masque in a letter of 8 January 1620, John Chamberlain observed that this "manner of running maske they pretend to borough from the French, (though for my part I remember no such thing in my time) but noe doubt but in all other fantasticall fashions so in this we strive to exceede and unstrip them."[8] Buckingham's "running masque" had clearly been an attempt to import a French style entertainment to the English court; although a popular success, it had equally clearly been, in the eyes of Chamberlain at least, a critical failure. Here was an opportunity for Doncaster, in the presence of the French ambassador and the leading French nobility, to show Buckingham and the court the proper way to handle a masque in the French manner.

The privilege of presenting a masque offered Doncaster another opportunity to offset the dominance of Buckingham:
Doncaster could choose the masquers. Sir John Finett informs
us that the masque was "presented by nine young Gentlemen, whereof the Lord *Montjoy*, and a Son of the Lord *Hollis*
were two *&c.*"[9] We are aware of Doncaster's preference for
using nine masquers, so their number is not surprising. What
is a little odd is their character: young gentlemen, not established courtiers. The former was Mountjoy Blount, later earl
of Newport, and the latter was a son of John Holles, first earl
of Clare. Both men appear to have been in Doncaster's service: one of the Holles boys had encountered him in Paris in
1616, and Blount would accompany him there on his embassy
of 1622.[10] The striking thing about these particular masquers
is that they were completely unknown—neither having, to
our knowledge, ever danced in a masque before. This marks a
radical departure from the regular roster of courtiers who
danced in the masques, a group that included Sir Henry Rich,
Sir George Goring, Sir Thomas Badger, Auchmouty, Aber-
crombie, and John Maynard.[11] These men had been dancing
in masques for years; they were established at court, and
were well known to the king. And this probably explains
Doncaster's decision not to employ them, and to use, in their
stead, a number of unknown and attractive young men from
his household—young men in need of an entrée. John Holles,
for example, was attempting to launch himself by standing
for a seat in the newly summoned Parliament. And Blount
was a popular athletic pinup boy in the early 1620s: Martin
Droeshout's engraving of him (figure 15) was apparently sold
as one of a series of engravings of young men framed by sport-
ing borders.[12] He would later dance in a number of the Caroline
masques.[13] We may presume that the other masquers were
young men of this ilk, and might imagine that Doncaster's
son was among their number.[14]

The logic of this decision may become clearer if we recall

Figure 15   Mountjoy Blount, by Martin Droeshout (*c.* 1626).
Reproduced by permission of the British Museum.

the legend that it was Doncaster who brought to the king's attention Robert Carr, Buckingham's predecessor as the leading favorite, by employing him as his proxy in the lists. He now had the chance to present a number of handsome young men from his entourage, one of whom might catch the royal eye (as Buckingham himself had done), and worm his way into the monarch's affections as Doncaster's creature.[15] This might seem farfetched; but we should not forget that Doncaster later employed his wife to exert her extraordinary sexual magnetism in order to ensnare King Charles, and that he may very well have used his daughter for similar purposes.[16]

The evening opened with Doncaster's masterpiece.[17] Simonds D'Ewes described it in his autobiography as "a most magnificent and profuse supper, which was seconded with a banquet, as was reported, which cost 500*l.* alone"—a widely circulated estimate.[18] The Venetian ambassador also remarked on the enormous cost of the evening.[19] The most substantial account is that of John Chamberlain, who elaborated upon its "sumptuous superfluitie" in a letter to Sir Dudley Carleton of 13 January:

> there were more then a 100 cookes (wherof forty were masters) set on worke for eight dayes before: the whole service was but six messe furnished with 1600 dishes, which were neither light nor sleight, but twelve fesants in a dish, fowre and twentie partridges, twelve dosen of larkes, *et sic de cæteris:* and for fish all that could be found far and neere, whole fresh salmons served by two and three in a dish, besides sixe or seven Muscovie salmons wherof some were above sixe foot long. Yt were to no purpose to recken up the grosser meates as two swannes in a dish, two chines of beefe, two pigges and the like; but yt is doubted this excessive spoyle will make a dearth of the choicest dainties, when this one supper consumed twelve score fesants baked, boyled, and rosted. After supper they had a banquet, then a maske, then a second banket, so that the sweet meats alone rising to 500[li] the whole charge is saide to be above 3000[li], besides sixe pound weight of amber-gris spent in cookerie valued at 300[li]. The King and Prince were present with the ambassadors at a table that went crosse the upper end of the long table, so that the King sitting in the midst had the full view of the whole companie and service; they supt in a lower gallerie. The maske was in a large roome above.[20]

Doncaster must have set out to exceed the entertainment of 1617: where that had featured 140 pheasants, this featured 240; where that involved 30 cooks, this involved 100; where that had cost £2200, this cost over £3000.[21] Jean Beaulieu pointed to its three strengths in a letter to William Trumbull of 11 January 1621: "quantitie, qualitie, & varietie."[22] In its quest for variety the supper was not selective so much as comprehensive: it did not merely pick choice examples of almost every edible creature from land, sea, and air (from the tiniest lark to the largest swan), it aimed to consume as many of each as possible—exhausting the available supply of luxuries from around the world in a single evening. In its use of huge quantities of ambergris as a culinary perfume, the Essex House entertainment sought to outdo the visitors in their own mode. The consumption of more than £300 worth of ambergris would surely affect the international markets, and would thus send just the right message back to Paris: Doncaster remained a force to be reckoned with.[23]

Performance

Having feasted and sampled the delicacies of the first banquet, Doncaster and his guests would have retired upstairs to the "large roome" set aside for the masque. Such retirement— often to the chamber adjoining the hall—was a traditional procedure in the case of an entertainment following a banquet, allowing, in this case, for the supper to be cleared and the second banquet set out.[24] From Chamberlain's remarks and a conjectural plan of Essex House in 1640 (figure 16), we may infer that the supper was held in the Low or Long Gallery on the third floor of the eastern extension of the house and the masque danced in the Great or High Gallery on the floor above it.[25] The plan shows a long, narrow room about 25 feet wide, while Ogilby and Morgan in their late seventeenth century plan depict one double that size (figure 17). The latter plan, astonishingly, would yield a masquing space barely inferior to that of the Whitehall Banqueting House itself; but if, as seems reasonable, we presume that the former gives a more accurate depiction of the layout in 1621, we would expect the gallery to have afforded a stage narrower by over a half, and presumably therefore also proportionately shallower, than the norm of 40 by 28 feet—a stage measured, most likely, in the teens.[26]

Whatever the precise size of the stage, the room could easily have been arranged in the traditional manner, with the

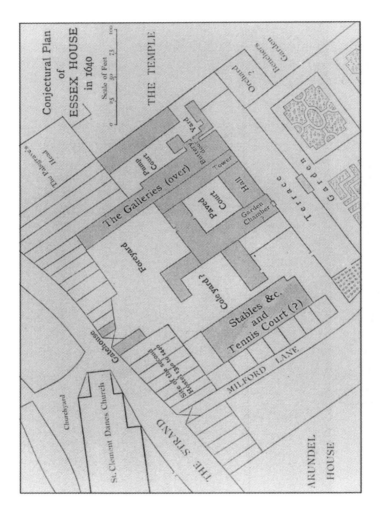

Figure 16   Conjectural plan of Essex House in 1640, by Charles Lethbridge Kingsford;
Archaeologia (1923). Reproduced by permission of the Society of Antiquaries, London.

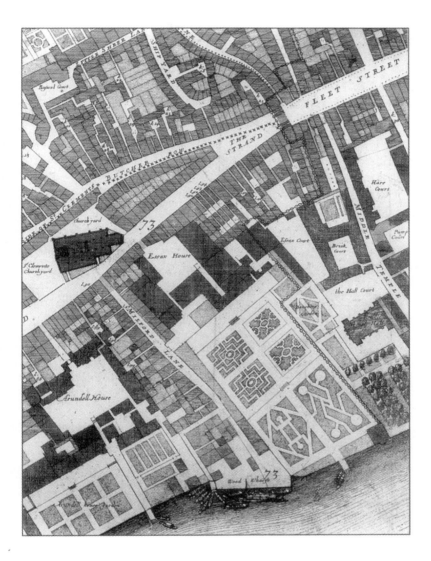

Figure 17 Plan of Essex House, from John Ogilby and William Morgan, *A Large and Accurate Map of the City of London* (1676). Reproduced by permission of the Guildhall Library, Corporation of London.

royal state facing the stage and dancing area, and the spectators arranged in seats around the walls. Once the king and his guests had taken up their proper places, a master of ceremonies representing the inventors and sponsor probably appeared to read or distribute copies of "The Argument," which explained the fable or conceit of the masque. This was a conventional prelude, employed by Jonson and other writers to counteract the fact that spectators often had very little idea what it was they were supposed to be watching.[27] Then the masque began.

Tellus (the earth-spirit), bent upon avenging the defeat of the Titans, vows to plague the gods with a new race of earthborn Giants. Confident of her success, she summons her creatures to a joyful holiday revel with a song: an unspecified number of antimasquers appear and dance (lines 18–34). The song mentions a tree, mines, a lion, an ape, a sheep, a boar, and a stag (although only the mines are referred to in the plural, we might presume, given the presentation of the dance as a revel, that the creatures danced in pairs—either by species, or, to emblematize the disorder of the dance, with one another). After the song and dance they all vanish and a cave appears, out of which rushes the second antimasque: a group of ".9. *giants the supposed sonnes and champions of the earth; warrelikely arrayed*" (lines 37–38). One of them delivers a lengthy speech threatening the beautiful young ladies in the audience (lines 62–64) and vowing vengeance, rape, and murder upon the gods (lines 40–83). A "*warrelike dance . . . performed to loud musicke*" follows, after which "*they . . . fall of by degrees, and clime to theire places*" (lines 84–86), beginning their assault upon the heavens. That assault is cut short by the entry of Pallas, who turns them to stone through the power of her Gorgon's head. "Thus I locke up your madnesse," she announces, as she goes about "Returninge Earth her one" (lines 88, 115). Pallas then delivers a speech justifying the reluctance of the gods to intervene in the rebellion. The gods, she claims, had intended to delay the operation of fate, allowing the rebels to run their course and repent of themselves, but the threat to such beauties among the spectators encouraged them to intervene. She warns the audience not to mistake clemency for weakness, reorders the stars, and then vanishes (lines 88–122). A second song is heard, warning any too-forward lover to expect a similar stony fate from his mistress's glance, thereby shifting the ground of the rebellion from the political to the sexual sphere (lines 124–43). What looked at first like an instance of political rebellion becomes an example of ill-mannered courtship. The second antimasque, which might be entitled "Giants Made Stone," is now over.

Those spectators familiar with the conventions of the court masque would have expected the revelation of the main masque to follow immediately, featuring a new setting and new performers. The situation here was similar to that of *The Golden Age Restored* (1616), in which Pallas had put paid to the rebellion of the Iron Age by turning the rebels to stone, and had then descended with Astraea as the scene changed. But something very unusual now takes place—something the conventional vocabulary of masque criticism, with its emphasis on the structural opposition of masque and antimasque, does not readily account for. After the song, Prometheus appears bearing his stolen fire: he comments on its heavenly origin, outlines its ingredients (including the lights of both sun and moon: both lust and chastity), and explains that he plans to use it to bring the petrified Giants to life as men, to "Deale soule into cold stone, and raise up man | Out of a punishment" (lines 175–76): to "beget | Obedient life; and manners . . . refine" (lines 177–78). In a breathtaking extension of the metamorphic technique employed in the earlier masques with which Doncaster was associated, the antimasquers are once more transformed. But this transformation is not to be achieved without assistance. As he makes his exit, Prometheus corrects the traditional version of the legend, and appeals for the approval and aid of the "Divinest powers" in the audience in raising life from the stones. After his departure a third song is heard, urging the spectators to look "with desire," and fan the heavenly fire with their breath. In a moment of potent magic, heightened by the accompaniment of music and light, the anti-masquers are revealed as the masquers, and Hermione-like, the stones begin to move.

The text is not specific about what exactly happens here, or about what, precisely, was represented in the main masque, but the absence of any accompanying explanation must mean that it was immediately identifiable and unambiguous. The conventional association of the number nine with the Worthies coincides with the appearance of the Worthies in a number of recent masques and with the impeccable character of the reformed antimasquers, to allow us to speculate that the main masque consisted of a tableau in which the masquers were "discovered," no doubt in a scene of light, as the Nine Worthies: those ancient heroes whom "the young world, | In her unstable youth, did then produce."[28] The text that precedes and accompanies the discovery suggests that the masquers are discovered as stones, statue-like in their immobility, and that they are gradually brought to life through the art of Prometheus and the power of the spectators. The gradual and visible animation of the statuesque masquers is (as we shall soon see) an essential part of the meaning of the masque.

The discovery of a masque of Worthies closely parallels that of Middleton's *Inner Temple Masque, or Masque of Heroes* (1619), in which nine *"Heroes deified for their virtues"* were discovered *"sitting in arches of clouds."*[29] The Essex House Worthies are not primarily presented as heroic warriors; they are beautiful, obedient, and well-mannered objects of desire— an adjustment that follows the presentation of the Giants' rebellion as a sexual transgression, and prepares the way for their dancing of the main masque and the revels. The main masque being danced, a fourth song "invites them to the

Ladyes" (line 216): invites the masquers to pick partners from the audience and dance the revels. Their performance of the measured steps of the dance expresses the smooth, harmonious operation of a universe governed once more by virtuous love (lines 217–34).

What the spectators at Essex House witnessed was not, as in *Lord Hay's Masque, The Lords' Masque,* or *Lovers Made Men,* a single transformation following an earlier, reported metamorphosis, but a double transformation: not "Lovers Made Men," but "Giants Made Stones Made Men." Doncaster had once more succeeded in providing "something *Novel,* neat, and unusual, that others might admire."

Sources

The masque possesses the philosophical seriousness and the elevated tone of the most dignified of the court masques; it is far removed from the whimsical inconsequence and bawdiness of the private theatricals. Its fable is manufactured from two distinct myths: the rebellion of the Giants against the gods, and the creation of man by Prometheus. While almost any Renaissance compendium of classical mythology might have served as a source for such material, the prime locus for the association of the two tales appears to be *The Library* of Apollodorus, where they are narrated in adjacent chapters (1.6–7). But no connection is there established between them other than the implied point that Prometheus was one of the Titans who had earlier rebelled against the gods—a point made more explicitly in the *Theogony* of Hesiod.

The treatment of the rebellion in the second antimasque reveals a further debt to the *Gigantomachia* of Claudian. In Apollodorus's version, Earth was so angered by the gods' treatment of the Titans, her offspring, that with the aid of Coelus she produced the Giants to wreak her revenge; the gods with the help of Hercules then defeated them. From Claudian is imported the creation of the Giants by Earth alone, the use of the name "Tellus" to refer to her, and the Giants' defeat by Pallas, using the Gorgon's head. The masque also imitates from Claudian Tellus's rousing speech to the Giants prior to their attack, a loose variation of which is placed in the mouth of one of the Giants themselves.[30]

An iconographic analogue, if not actually a source, for Pallas's petrifaction of the Giants may be found in Barthelemy Aneau's *Picta Poesis* (Lyon, 1552), which includes an emblem showing Pallas turning men to stone with the Gorgon's head— stupefying them through the combined force of arms and let-ters (figure 7).[31] The employment of this trope in the masque is heavily indebted to Jonson's use of Pallas and her shield to crush the rebellion of the Iron Age in *The Golden Age Re-stored*—a scene which was itself closely based upon Claudian's *Gigantomachia*.[32] At the time of *The Essex House Masque*, moreover, Pallas and the Gorgon's head, and possibly the Gigantomachy, were icons of some topicality at court.

During the winter of 1620–21, Anthony Van Dyck was in London, engaged upon projects for the king.[33] During this pe-riod he was working on *The Continence of Scipio*, a painting that entered the collection of the marquess of Buckingham, and which appears to represent Buckingham in the figure of the bridegroom (figure 18). In the lower left corner of this paint-ing is a fragment of a classical frieze depicting two Gorgon heads (a third adorns a ewer on its lower right side): these heads, with their Minervan associations, clearly allude to the moral and political wisdom of the continent Scipio, who chose to restore a captured bride to her betrothed. In 1972 the very frieze fragment depicted in the painting was discovered dur-ing building work on the site of Arundel House, the residence of Lord Arundel, and home to his collection of antique sculp-ture (figures 13, 19, 20).[34] The discovery prompted a debate over the ownership of the frieze and the commissioning of

Figure 18 Anthony Van Dyck, *The Continence of Scipio*
(1620–21). Reproduced by courtesy of the Governing Body, Christ Church, Oxford.

Figure 19   Thomas Howard, earl of Arundel, by Daniel Mytens
(*c.* 1616). Reproduced by permission of the National Portrait
Gallery, London.

Figure 20   Gorgons; fragment of a Roman frieze, Antonine period;
Museum of London. Reproduced by permission of His Grace, the
Duke of Norfolk.

the portrait—a debate that remains unresolved.[35] For our purposes the value of the frieze lies in the fact that it was clearly
a curiosity at court at the time of the masque, and was incorporated into a painting which spoke to the politics of the period.[36] Just how it did so is arguable; but it seems certain that
it appealed to the royal self-presentation, in which the monarch was figured in Minervan terms.[37] More precisely, in its
representation of Scipio restoring the captured bride, virtue
intact, to her betrothed, the painting appears to allude to the
king's part in securing the agreement of the Manners family
to a match between Buckingham and their daughter, Katherine, in the summer of 1620.[38] There may, moreover, be an
allusion in the three Gorgon heads to the foreign policy of
the period. In his 1609 account of the central classical myths,
Bacon had interpreted the legend of Perseus and Medusa as a
lesson in the handling of warfare: Perseus's journey implied a

warning against attacking neighbouring states; his success suggested the need for a just cause in warfare; and the fact that Perseus attacked the only mortal one of the three Gorgons implied a warning against embarking upon wars which could not be won.[39] Such a message would have offered confirmation and support for James's wary approach to the Bohemian problem.

Contemporary understanding of the provenance of the frieze sheds further light upon the genesis and topicality of the fable of *The Essex House Masque*. Among those who saw the frieze at Arundel House (although we do not know when) was Lord Arundel's longstanding associate in the study of antiquities, Inigo Jones, who noted in the margin of his copy of Vitruvius that "the Antike freeze with gorgons heads" came from "the temble of Pallas" in Smyrna: an identification which brings out the Minervan associations implicit in Van Dyck's portrait.[40] The temple to which Jones refers was the Trajeneum at Pergamon, from which Arundel acquired additional frieze fragments depicting the Gigantomachy—the very topic animated in the first part of *The Essex House Masque*.[41] Although we should perhaps attribute Arundel's acquisition of these fragments to the efforts of his indefatigable agent William Petty in the mid-1620s, it is clear from Van Dyck's painting that at least one fragment thought to come from the temple was known at court by the winter of 1620, as was its Minervan context: it is therefore possible that its depiction of the Gigantomachy was also known.[42]

The second part of *The Essex House Masque* concerns the creation of man by Prometheus. The version of the legend presented here is highly unusual. In the masque Prometheus creates man not from clay but from rock—the very stone into which the Giants had earlier been transformed. This is an Orphic Prometheus, an Amphion who, to the accompaniment of music, makes stones to move; as a motif, it inverts the wild, anti-Orphic revel of Tellus. The use of such a figure may have been prompted by the appearance of Orpheus in Buckingham's masque of the previous winter, in which he had lamented the loss of Eurydice with the exclamation: "I would Transforme the rest to Stoanes."[43] There may be an iconographic context for the device in an illustration frequently reproduced in early Italian editions of Ovid's *Metamorphoses*, which depicts Prometheus raising man from a rock (figure 9).[44] But there is also perhaps a jokingly competitive compliment to Arundel, whose growing collection of antique sculpture was housed in the long gallery at the nearby Arundel House (figure 19). This reference suggests that, while Arundel's gallery may have contained an impressive array of ancient statues, Doncaster's, by contrast, contained stones that could dance. As a conceit for a masque, the animation of petrified figures is probably indebted most directly to *The Lords' Masque* of Campion and Jones (1613), which had featured the animation of eight *"women-statues"* through the agency of Prometheus and his heavenly fire.[45] The French *Ballet des Argonautes* (1614) had, however, featured rocks (men thus transformed by the enchantress, Circe) moving at the sound of Amphion's music, and yielding up dancers to the king and queen.[46]

A further variant on the myth, amounting to a full-scale revision, lies in Prometheus's search for divine approval for his use of the heavenly fire. Contemporary mythographers and masque writers were keen to present Prometheus as a figure of wisdom rather than rebellion, as a benefactor who introduced divine wisdom to humanity (and paid the price through his continued torture).[47] In *The Lords' Masque*, Campion and Jones had even gone so far as to associate Prometheus with the Worthies by presenting him *"attyred as one of the ancient Heroes."*[48] *The Essex House Masque*, however, takes such revisionism to its conclusion. Despite the implication in "The Argument" that the spectators are witnesses to an act of rebellion (lines 14–16), Prometheus's action, though undertaken furtively and against the wishes of the gods (lines

146–51), is here ultimately given divine sanction (that of the royal spectators), as a result of Prometheus's assurance that "the life I give | Shall weare in servinge you by whom I live" (lines 184–85); incredibly, Prometheus himself goes unpunished. This is no dramatic oversight, but a stunning reversal: "The Argument" reminds the spectators of the conventional interpretation of the legend, thus priming them for the astonishing revision to come. In retrospect, it becomes clear that the warning offered in "The Argument" that man "never should aspire | To such forbidden height" refers not to the work of Prometheus, but to the rebellion of the Giants.

Fable

In its blending of the Gigantomachy with the revised myth of Prometheus, the masque deftly manufactures a new fable—a fable, it may be added, of considerable intellectual coherence. Its thesis might be expressed as "obedience through wisdom and love." This thesis operates on both macrocosmic and microcosmic levels, as a fully integrated natural, moral, and political allegory.

In the wild and discordant dance presented in the first antimasque we witness the rampant disorderliness of mere nature, liberated from divine control. In the second antimasque we move from disorder to outright rebellion. The natural philosophical context is provided by Natalis Comes in his account of the Titans:

> Quidam elementorum mutationes per hanc fabulam explicasse antiquos crediderunt, ac Titanes vocarunt illa elementa, quae terrestre quiddam & crastum intra se continerent, quae vi corporum superiorum inferius assidue detrudantur. Nam vapores semper sursum vi solis attrahuntur, qui vbi ad superiora peruenerint, virtute diuinorum corporum vel soluuntur in purissima elementa, vel repelluntur inferius, quae dimicatio est sempiterna . . .[49]

Certain ones believed that the ancients explained the muta-
tion of elements by this fable, naming Titans those elements
which contained within themselves anything earthy and dense,
which are continually driven downwards by the force of supe-
rior bodies. For exhalations are always attracted upward by the
virtue of the sun, which, when they arrive at the upper regions,
are either dissolved by the power of the divine bodies into the
most refined elements or pushed back lower, which struggle is
perpetual.

That the Giants are to be seen as terrestrial exhalations akin
to, though not identical with, an earthquake (line 28) is suggested by Tellus, in her injunction to the hollows of the earth
to move (line 27). George Sandys noted a similar reading of
the Gigantomachy as a volcanic eruption: "the Gyants are
those windes that struggle in the cavernes of the Earth; which
not finding a way inforce it; vomiting fire, and casting up stones
against heaven or *Jupiter*."[50] It follows from these readings
that Pallas's assertion that the rebellion would have burned
itself out in its own good time was well grounded in contemporary natural philosophy. The Giants, as exhalations of earth,
attracted by the power of the sun, are consigned to the region
of air. On meeting the borders of the heavens (represented by
Pallas) they are pushed back to earth, cooling and petrifying
in the process, and forming mountains. Their assault is doomed
to fail.[51] The celestial fire of Prometheus creates man from
rock by purging it of the dross of earth, its grosser elements
(extreme density, moistness, and coldness), and inspiring it
with the animating heat and light of the heavens. The result
is not a complete purgation of the material, but an apt balance between the terrestrial and the divine.

Prometheus is not concerned just to animate the stones; he
is also concerned to explain, for the benefit of the audience,
the several ingredients of the stolen fire. His list expresses the
harmony of natural and supernatural, super- and sublunary
heat and light compounded in the fire. It also reveals the extent to which the masque is steeped in neoplatonic learning.

These ingredients are enumerated in descending order, moving from the circumference toward the center of the Ptolemaic universe. Prometheus ranges from the fixed stars, to the sun, then to the planet Venus, and next to the moon. Moving below the sphere of the moon, he enumerates various meteorological phenomena associated with the regions of fire and air: comets (a question is raised about their precise location), thunderbolts, shooting stars, and sparks—phenomena associated with the aerial region, traditionally thought to be governed by Juno (this is the meaning of the reference to the "sparkes of Junoes Jealousy" in line 173).[52] The soul is thus composed, in Platonic fashion, of heat and light both material and spiritual, the former serving to allay the purity of the latter.[53] Those ingredients are harmoniously blended astrological influences. The excessive heat and dryness of the sun are tempered by the moisture and coolness of "the chast | Light of the winter moone" (lines 166–67). Similarly, the benign influence of Venus offsets the malignity of Mars. The reference to "the lusting lookes of Venus, by which shee | Intreated Mars first to Adultery" (lines 164–65) should be read not morally but astrologically: Venus's "lusting lookes" are those influences by which, in favorable aspect, she attracts Mars. Her coolness, moisture, and temperateness balance his heat, dryness, and ardor; together they fuse the masculine and feminine principles, yielding a harmonious blend of qualities, especially suited to love and procreation.[54] As Leone Ebreo put it: "although the heat of Mars is excessive in ardour, Venus with her sober coolness tempers and proportions him to these operations."[55] The result of all this mingling of qualities in the soul is the "moderate heat" with which Prometheus can create temperate life, mediating between the extreme ardor of the Giants and the extreme inertia of the stones. Earth, water, air, and fire are now happily blended.

The physical process thus described involves a moral

dimension. In the moral sphere, the opening antimasque displays the human psyche ungoverned by divine love and wisdom. It affords a grotesque inversion of the conventional image of Orpheus charming rocks, trees, and beasts with his song (figure 21)—an image taken to refer to the calming of passions by music.[56] This image had earlier been enacted in a harmonious dance of beasts in *The Lords' Masque*.[57] Rather than calming the passions, however, Tellus whips them up, and the hint of golden-age harmoniousness in the lion's dancing with the lamb (or sheep), only emphasizes the topsy-turvy quality of the revel. Traditional number and animal symbolism underscore the materiality of the revelers. The five beasts named as dancers may allude to the five senses. Four of those named were, moreover, conventionally connected with the four temperaments and their associated elements: the lion (fire), the ape (air), the lamb (water), and the pig (earth)—though here it is a boar. The rebellion of the Giants was widely conflated with that of the Titans and taken to signify the oppression of knowledge and virtue by the gross, material body.[58] Pallas was conventionally thought to represent divine wisdom, the power of which was expressed by the Gorgon's head on her shield.[59] Her ability to quash native instincts led to her depiction as the guardian of virgins.[60] Her defeat of the Giants thus represented the triumph of divine wisdom or reason over material appetite, and the power of virginity over lust.[61] The action of Prometheus brings the masque to its conclusion by illustrating the infusion of wisdom and love into the body by means of the soul.[62] This was a conventional reading: according to George Sandys, for example, "*Prometheus* signifies Providence, and *Minerva* Heavenly Wisdome: by Gods providence therefore and wisdome Man was created. The celestiall fire is his soule inspired from above."[63] The peculiar character of this Prometheus, moreover, establishes a precisely pointed relationship between the anti-Orphic Tellus and the

186 *Orphei Musica.*

Ad eundem.

L O, O R P H E V S with his harpe, that sauage kinde did tame:
The Lions fierce, and Leopardes wilde, and birdes about him came.
For, with his muficke fweete, their natures hee fubdu'de:
But if wee thinke his playe fo wroughte, our felues wee doe delude.
For why? befides his fkill, hee learned was, and wife:
And coulde with fweetenes of his tonge, all fortes of men fuffice.
And thofe that weare moft rude, and knewe no good at all:
And weare of fierce, and cruell mindes, the worlde did brutifhe call.
Yet with perfuafions founde, hee made their hartes relente,
That meeke, and milde they did become, and followed where he wente.
Lo thefe, the Lions fierce, thefe, Beares, and Tigers weare:
The trees, and rockes, that lefte their roomes, his muficke for to heare.
But, you are happie moft, who in fuche place doe ftaye: [playe.
You neede not T H R A C I A feeke, to heare fome impe of O R P H E V S
Since, that fo neare your home, Apollos darlinge dwelles;
Who L I N V S, & A M P H I O N ftaynes, and O R P H E V S farre excelles.
For, hartes like marble harde, his harmonie dothe pierce:
And makes them yeelding paffions feele, that are by nature fierce.
But, if his muficke faile: his curtefie is fuche,
That none fo rude, and bafe of minde, but hee reclaimes them muche.
Nowe fince you, by deferte, for both, commended are:
I choofe you, for a Iudge herein, if truthe I doe declare.
And if you finde I doe, then ofte therefore reioyce:
And thinke, I woulde fuche neighbour haue, if I might make my choice.

In fta-

Horat. Art. poët.
Sylueftres homines fa-
cer interprefq̃, deorum,
Cædibus & fœdo victu
deterruit Orpheus;
Dictus ob hoc lenire ti-
gres, rapidofq̃. leones.

E. P. Efquier.

Propert. lib. 1. de
Lino.
Tunc ego fim Inachio
notior arte Lino.
De Amphione Ho-
rat. in Art. poët.
Dictus & Amphion
Thebanæ conditor vrbis
Saxa mouere fono te-
ftudinis, & prece blanda
Ducere quò vellet, &c.

Figure 21 Orpheus controlling the passions; from Geffrey
Whitney, *A Choice of Emblemes* (1586). Reproduced by
permission of the Folger Shakespeare Library.

Orphic Prometheus, just as the divine wisdom of Pallas opposed the earthy irrationality of Tellus. Such relationships express the philosophical coherence of the masque.

The political significance of the fable emerges from its natural and moral meanings. The Giants are rebels: "too potent subjects," as Sandys put it, "or the tumultuary vulgar; rebelling against their Princes, called Gods, as his substitutes: who by their disloyaltie and insolencies violate all lawes both of God and man, and profane whatsoever is sacred."[64] They are drawn by the attractive light of the royal sun to the forbidden reaches of the sky; deluded by the sun's power into dreaming of an existence beyond their proper sphere.[65] Their defeat by Pallas represents the inevitable triumph of royal wisdom, and the reestablishment of the natural political order. Rebellion is thus shown to be an inevitable but temporary byproduct of virtuous rule.

A glance at these complementary lines of interpretation makes it clear why the myth of Prometheus should be so readily blended with that of the rebellion of the Giants. In marrying the two myths what has the poet done other than tease out a latent symbolic connection between them? In depicting the creation of man from the petrified Giants, the masque retains its commitment to the view that Prometheus fashioned man out of earth, for that is what the Giants are ("*sonnes and champions of the earth*," lines 37–38). In restoring them to life through the infusion into the terrestrial body of a divine soul, Prometheus completes the work of Pallas (with whom he is conventionally associated), so redeeming earth and thereby producing the civilized, obedient, semidivine race of men (lines 177–86). The masquers' dancing with the ladies in the audience expresses the ordering power of divine love: what they had earlier uncivilly attempted (through their assault on the gods and their attempted rape of Pallas), they now lawfully achieve. And their dancing guarantees the continued realization of such plenitude, for the divine fire is rekindled by every lady's touch (lines 223–28), and any potential vacuum is immediately filled by the dancers who, through their motion, merge with the music to become part of the heavenly harmony—"A paire | Like aire" (lines 231–32).[66]

Structure

In its structure and spectacle, the masque builds upon the strengths of earlier Doncastrian productions. While *Lord Hay's Masque* had, with its elaborate scene changes and fantastic costumes, been a triumph of spectacle, its dramatic construction was not as elegantly economical as that of *Lovers Made Men*. But what the later masque gained in coherence it lost in spectacle, lacking even a rudimentary scene change. *The Essex House Masque* attempts to outdo these earlier masques; and it does so without losing the structural economy of *Lovers Made Men*. This achievement is made possible by an unprecedented spectacular innovation: the Doncastrian signature of transforming the antimasquers is used here not once, but twice. The establishment of a credible intellectual and dramatic connection between those two transformations yields a coherent action.

The careful disposition of the parts of the masque reveals a confident and innovative handling of generic convention, and a sensitive response to the constraints and opportunities of the occasion. Its arrangement of parts offers variety within repetition:

> Song + Dance (First antimasque)
> Speech + Dance (Second antimasque)
> Speech (Pallas)
> Song
> Speech (Prometheus)
> Song + Dance (Main masque)
> Song + Dance (Revels)

As an interlude between two banquets, the masque needed to be brief; as a prelude to the revels it needed to introduce dancing as an expression of lawful love. The latter requirement is met by the transformation of the performers from fighters to lovers, and therefore dancers (dancing being an expression of the universal ordering power of love). The former is satisfied by the dramatic economy of the masque, and by the exploitation of a structural consequence of the use of the same performers throughout. Instead of performing the usual three masque dances (entry, main dance, and revels), the masquers perform only a main dance that leads directly to the revels.[67] This elegant compression helps to unify the action by underscoring the point that the second antimasque is in this case the masquers' entry. It also expresses in structural terms the philosophical balance between the two worlds of the masque, with the two masque dances mirroring the two antimasques. Such mirroring extends to the careful balancing of complimentary parts of the masque. The structural antithesis between the rebellious speech of the Giant and the restorative speech of Prometheus is reinforced by the fact the two speeches are of identical length (each is 44 lines long).

Mirroring is, however, too static a term to suggest the fluidity of movement involved in the masque, which exhibits not a static opposition, but a unified progression from the world of the antimasque to that of the masque. It transcends the condition of argument and approaches that of narrative. The narrative proper begins with the entry dance of the Giants; it pivots on their petrifaction by Pallas; and is requited by their subsequent animation by Prometheus. The fact that Tellus's antimasque was not fully integrated into the narrative was noticed by contemporaries, one of whom appeared to regard it as an independent attraction, claiming that the evening's entertainment consisted of a feast "accompanied with a danse, a maske, & a banquet."[68] Perhaps the text's reference to the first antimasquers as "Antemaskers," and the absence of any description of the Giants is significant, suggesting that the first dance is merely an ante-masque: a dance before the masque.[69] But the first "Antemaske" is nonetheless, like the antimasques of Jonson, fully integrated into the broad thematic and structural sweep of the entertainment, with its movement toward the revels. This movement is clearly signaled by Tellus's topsy-turvy presentation of her antimasque as a victory revel (like Jonson's *Oberon*, this masque begins and ends with a revel).[70] The entertainment opens with the animation of stones by Tellus (the mines of the first antimasque) and it concludes with the animation of stones by Prometheus. The action moves from macrocosmic disorder (Tellus's illegitimate and premature holiday "revell," involving nature's creatures) to microcosmic rebellion (the Giants' rebellion), through the creation of microcosmic order (the petrifaction and reanimation of the Giants) to the establishment of macrocosmic order (the revels proper, in which the dancing of masquers and spectators communicates the newfound harmony to the court and, by implication, the country at large). It might be expressed thus:

Antirevel—Antimasque—Transformation |
Transformation—Masque—Revel.

The amatory trajectory here established was continued beyond the revels in the second banquet, which made lavish use of the aphrodisiac ambergris, from which Venus was reputedly born.[71]

The masque thus appears, in typically Doncastrian manner, to be triadic in structure. A three-step counter movement answers a three-stage opening movement. This triadic principle permeates the masque. Three speakers deliver three speeches at key points in the narrative; that narrative is punctuated by songs. Although there are four, rather than three, songs, the two masque songs (those that accompany the revelation of the masque and the revels) each possess three stanzas and feature three rhymes. As a structuring unit of the cosmos, the triad gives rise to the number nine in which the Giants and ultimately the Worthies appear.[72] In such a context, the number nine is auspicious in that it suggests both the created universe (with its nine spheres) and the human soul (with its nine senses) and the perfect end of effort (in that it is the last of the digits). It suggests, in sum, the plenitude of creation, brought to fruition by Prometheus.[73]

The retention of the same performers as both Giants and Worthies contributes to the unity of the narrative, as does the construction of roles appropriate to their dignities. While their status might prohibit courtiers from taking speaking roles or appearing in the antimasques of official court productions, in private theatricals they frequently did so.[74] Even in private, however, there were limits to the kind of roles they might adopt: the ghostly lovers of *Lovers Made Men* are victims and not, like the Giants of *The Essex House Masque*, rebels. But young gentlemen without official court positions might, on account of their insignificance and relative anonymity, be given greater liberty in role-playing: they might be presented as rebels and then reformed. The precise character of that reformation is once again an index of the liberty of the occasion, demonstrating the extent to which the inventors of *The Essex House Masque* were not bound to regard the occasion as an official court masque. As in *Lovers Made Men*, the movement of the masque is a moderate one. The masquers are made men, not gods; the masque moves toward mortal perfection.

Spectators

Although the question of why the masque settles for so moderate a movement may in part be answered by reference to the dignities of the performers, it must also be explained by reference to the way in which the masque responds to and makes use of its spectators. The difficulty here was that although the masque was not presented at court, and could not therefore command the full political and aesthetic weight of an official production, the king was nonetheless present; he could not be ignored. But nor would it be appropriate to center the entire fiction upon him. Doncaster's reception of the embassy was, from the king's point of view, designed to offer unofficial encouragement to the French to advance their marriage proposals without revealing his own involvement in doing so to the Spanish. The inventors finessed this problem with considerable success. Like *Lovers Made Men*, the transformation of antimasquers into masquers is effected not by direct appeal to the royal presence, but by the action of agents internal to the fiction: Pallas petrifies the rebels and Prometheus animates them. Such agents needed to be figures of sufficient weight to impel the transformations, and that weight is generated in part by their mythic associations and in part by their conventional association with King James. Pallas was widely associated with his wisdom, while the "Promethean fire" of his gaze had been celebrated by Jonson in *The Masque of Beauty*. But for all that Pallas and Prometheus might be associated with the monarch, they could not, given his presence in the audience, be completely identified with him (even James could not be both spectator *and* participant). The masque could not therefore rely exclusively upon these conventional associations to provide the justification for its actions.

Given the gender and character of the masquers, it was only apt that the masque should, in its construction of a suitable impetus for the unfolding action, exploit the presence of ladies in the audience. The appearance of Pallas is attributed to the gods' concern for the gathered "Glories" of the court, those fragile beauties who (unlike the gods themselves) are threatened by the intrusion of the lustful rebels. The narrative aptness of this impetus may be gauged by contrasting it with *The*

Golden Age Restored, in which Pallas permits the rebellion of the Iron Age to unfold, and appears only when she decides it is time for the rebels to learn that their adversaries are unconquerable: "'Twas time t<o>'appeare, and let their follies see | 'Gainst whom they fought and with what destinee" (lines 73–74).[75] In *The Golden Age Restored,* Pallas's behavior is motivated solely by the dramatist's desire to express a philosophical point;[76] in *The Essex House Masque* that point is prompted by the logic of the occasion—by a just interlocking of the spectators with the fiction.

The credit for the animation of the stony Giants is divided between the art of Prometheus and the power of the spectators. Although his artistry and stolen fire impel the transformation, the masque asserts that art alone is insufficiently powerful to complete it. Prometheus appeals to the "Divinest powers" in the audience to "spare a saving glaunce | This worke of life to reskue; if mischaunce | Dare to attempt it" (lines 186–88). While this appears to offer the spectators only a limited, watchdog role in the process, their centrality is underscored both by Prometheus's departure from the stage prior to the transformation, and by the song announcing it—a song that presumably represents Prometheus's art in operation. The song requires the audience to "Calmely looke and with desire | Ad to the fire," on the grounds that "all the art | Cannot impart | So much thereof as you" (lines 192–93, 196–98). As the masque is discovered, the song remarks: "Then veiw the spring of man begun | By your one sun" (lines 208–09). What is this life-giving sun?

A productive ambiguity is at work here, which depends upon the openendedness of the referent. Is this sun something every member of the audience possesses? Or is it something singular? The image of the sun is conventionally associated with the eyes. In this respect two different yet complementary sources are implied. Read in a Petrarchan context, the image suggests the life- or death-giving eyes of the beautiful ladies in the audience—the "Divinest powers" to whom Prometheus appeals for support in his quest, and in whose service the newly created lovers will expend themselves. A device of this sort was employed in the French *ballet, Les Fées de la Forest de Saint-Germain* (1625), in which men begin to dance "comme des demy-Dieux" due to the magical gaze of the ladies in the audience.[77] But there was another conventional source for such glances—a source that could be implied but not named. In the Jacobean court masque, the impetus for the transformation was invariably the monarch, whose gaze, in the language of Jacobean kingship (absolutist in tone, if not in fact), gave or withdrew life: "So breakes the sunne earths rugged chaines, | Wherein rude winter bound her vaines," comments the song accompanying the transformation of the Irish ambassadors in *The Irish Masque* (lines 187–88).[78] The ladies of the court are not, then, the only ones invited to gaze with desire on the young men performing the masque. The suggestion is not explicit—that would be unthinkably tactless—but it is hinted at in the openended language of the discovery song. The spectators—male monarch and female beauties—are thus dramatically integrated into the action of the masque. They are the impetus for the transformation, which they impel by doing exactly what spectators do naturally—by gazing. The lighting effects accompanying the discovery no doubt demonstrated visually the implicit assertion that heavenly love on earth flows directly from the heart of the Jacobean court, which alone has the power to transform depraved and rebellious monsters into the greatest heroes.

But how, exactly, does the gaze of the spectators help Prometheus to animate the stones? To answer this question, we turn once more to the neoplatonic background of the masque. In order to aid the animation, the spectators are invited to gaze with desire on the masquers, but they are warned to do so calmly:

Calmely looke and with desire
  Ad to the fire
Which your breathinges must fan higher

(lines 192–94)

This is an important injunction. Although the medium of sight was, in Ficinian terms, one of the most refined and elevated of the senses, it was still a sense; inadequately regulated, it could prompt an appetite to satisfy the baser senses—could lead, that is, to the depravity of lust.[79] This was what had happened when the Giants saw the beauties of the audience: "no beauty, which youre eyes | Have mark'd content in, but shall proove a prize," crowed the lead Giant (lines 62–63).[80] In yet another of the masque's structural parallelisms, the very beauties once threatened by the Giants in the antimasque become the means of the Giants' redemption in the masque. Those beauties are asked to gaze on the masquers calmly, and with desire or, in other words, with love. In neoplatonic terms, this is a natural process: beauty inspires the desire that is love.[81] The once monstrous Giants, now possessed of a divine soul (the Promethean fire), have become virtuous and therefore beautiful. Love is aroused by the spectators' apprehension of that beauty.[82] Their love is then expressed, still through the medium of sight, to the beloved.

But why is this necessary to Prometheus's project? Prometheus is concerned lest the heavenly fire be extinguished. He has good reason for concern. The celestial fire has been dragged down to earth from its proper sphere, and is to be merged not even with a beast—as in a regular human birth—but with its opposite—with cold, heavy, and inert stone.[83] There is a real danger that the stone might prove too recalcitrant for the fire, expunging it. Here the spectators assist, not merely by fanning it with their breath but, more importantly, by stimulating through their gaze a motion to love and therefore heat on the part of the masquers.[84] This is a vital contribution to the animation because Prometheus's quest to vivify the stones through the celestial fire of the soul is nothing more than the stimulation in them of this same motion toward the good, the divine.[85] The spectators therefore bring the masque to fruition by following their own natures: by gazing lovingly, and with beauty, on the handsome young masquers who return their gaze.

The language of neoplatonic philosophy affords principles to account for this animation of the Giants; but when stones start to move, we know we are in the presence of magic. The only question is—magic of what kind? It has sometimes been suggested that the court entertainments of the Renaissance exhibited a species of astral magic described at length in the third book of Ficino's *De Triplici Vita*. In such magic, the operator harnessed favorable planetary influences through charms and talismans, gems and odors, through spells and musical incantations.[86] Dame Frances Yates argued that the "Magnificences" staged in Paris in 1581 were in fact "a vast moving talisman, formed of figures in different colours moving amongst incantatory scenes designed to draw down favourable influences on the French monarchy."[87] She and her followers have advanced the same view of the English court masque; but it has not commanded universal assent.[88] Stephen Orgel objects that contemporary commentators tended to account for masques in rational or scientific terms; he suggests that we read them as models or metaphors for the natural and supernatural forces they imitate.[89] *The Essex House Masque* does not provide evidence to settle this debate. We know too little about its performance—about the tone of its music, the shape of its dances, the color of its costumes—to be certain how far it might have been constructed as a talisman. But that some attempt—or at least an allusion to the attempt—to draw down astral forces takes place in the masque seems certain. Pallas concludes her speech by calling on the disordered stars to rearrange themselves in favorable aspects:

shine agen
Not cold; and carelessly; but so as when
You courted Nature in your youth; and gave
Thankfull aspects for those faire lookes you have.

(lines 119–22)

In his account of the ingredients of his heavenly fire, Prometheus refers to Venus in her benign aspect countering and attracting Mars: "The lusting lookes of Venus, by which shee | Intreated Mars first to Adultery" (lines 164–65). The reference to Mars seems slightly gratuitous until we contemplate the positions of the stars at the time of the masque and discover that Mars had just entered Scorpio, his mansion, and was thus set to exercise his most malign influence for the coming months.[90] That this may be an actual appeal to Venus to offset that malignity by adopting a benign aspect on Mars is thus a tantalizing possibility—especially given the fact that Venus was, at the time of the masque, not in favorable aspect with Mars. Perhaps the employment of ambergris in the evening's entertainment should also be seen in this light, as a further attempt to offset the malignity of Mars through its solar and jovial resonances?[91] Is it possible that the numerological structure of the masque also possesses a talismanic dimension? These are tantalizing prospects, but we lack sufficient evidence to explore them.

If a masque should be judged by the extent to which it unifies its disparate elements into a coherent fiction and breaks down the barrier between performers and spectators, integrating them into a single awe-inspiring action, *The Essex House Masque* must be allowed to stand high in the annals of achievement. Its spectacular effects—dancing trees, opening caves, masquers coming to life—may have been conventional, but rarely were they so admirably woven together into a single, coherent fable as here. It can stand alongside the unperformed *Neptune's Triumph* as a model for the genre.[92] One might object that the moderateness of its movement—toward humanity, rather than divinity—deprives it of the overwhelming emotional power of the greatest court masques. Perhaps. One has to concede, however, that few works combine so delicately, with such narrative aptness, that extraordinary blend of light, music, poetry, and motion, which defines the Stuart court masque.

Politics

The masque was not, of course, a purely aesthetic construct; it was also a diplomatic intervention, and as such it should also be assessed. As an official, diplomatic entertainment the masque had to communicate several different, not entirely compatible, messages to the various spectators at which it was aimed. It involved transactions between the king and the French; between the king and the absent Spaniards; between Doncaster and the king; and between Doncaster and his rivals at court. It was, in addition, employed by its inventors to conduct their own literary and political negotiations with rival masque writers. These several imperatives create a complex web of signification that we must attempt to disentangle.

On behalf of the king and court, *The Essex House Masque* gives the French ambassador and his monarch a lesson in how to deal with rebellion—a lesson that would, given the presentation of the Huguenots as rebellious Giants or Titans in contemporary French court poetry and entertainments, have been quite clear.[93] The masque's reliance upon Pallas rather than Hercules to defeat the Giants makes the point that rebellion may be crushed by wisdom rather than force; the use of force implies a meanness of stature and a tenuous grasp on power: "Are gods so lowe condicion'd: not to bee | Or knowne or feard; but by their Tyranny," inquires Pallas (lines 96–97). The appropriate response of those as secure in their power as the gods would have been to do nothing (the weighty, earthly Giants have no chance of reaching the heavens): only when this approach seems to endanger the gathered beauties of the court does Pallas step in. The presentation of the rebellion in sexual terms suggests that the underlying cause of political insubordination is not desire for power so much as a misguided desire for love: it may therefore be cured by a return of affection. And the restoration of life through an infusion of divine love suggests that while wisdom may halt rebellion, it cannot alone produce obedient behavior. Pallas does not create; she destroys, producing only sterile immobility. It is a similar point to that made by Jonson in *The Golden Age Restored*, in which Pallas points out to Astraea that, without the restoration of love, the golden age is only half restored (lines 178–80).[94] Neither force nor wisdom alone, then, but wisdom joined with love are the appropriate tools for dealing with the Huguenot problem.

By introducing the Worthies—figures who had been employed in recent masques for their militant Protestant associations—the masque communicates England's ability to take a tough stance in defense of Protestantism abroad, without actually doing so: the Worthies are presented as lovers and dancers, and not primarily as warriors.[95] The masque thus avoids any explicit endorsement of military action, while simultaneously implying that it might, under certain circumstances (when it is undertaken by those who have been duly instructed by love and wisdom), be appropriate. As such, it communicates the wavering royal line to the French in regard to the Huguenots, and to the Spanish in regard to the Palatinate.

The presentation in the main masque of nine specimens of fine English manhood as reformed lovers is also an oblique come-on to the French in respect to their marriage proposal. It is oblique in that it manages to avoid flagrancy (and the risk of offending the Spanish) by its exclusion of the prince from the masque (that would have been too blatant). Indeed, the very fact that the masque is offered by men rather than women is, given the all-male composition of the French embassy, rather striking. Rather than featuring English ladies for the French visitors to dance with, it invites the French to contemplate the grace and decorum of contemporary English courtship. The masque itself offers the proof of that decorum. In its focus upon love and lust, order and rebellion, in its concern with the appropriate relationship of love and valor, with its blend of mythological and chivalric themes, and, in particular, in the centrality of its metamorphoses, the masque employs the symbolic language and speaks to the concerns of contemporary French *ballets*, especially those sponsored by Cadenet's brother—the court favorite, Luynes. Indeed, *The Essex House Masque* does not merely respond to the *ballets*, it outdoes them. While Luynes's recent *Délivrance de Persée* had hinged upon the appearance of Louis as Godfrey of Bulloigne, *The Essex House Masque* introduces not just Godfrey, but all nine of the Worthies. And, while several *ballets* had featured the retransformation of metamorphosed figures, *The Essex House Masque* presents not one but two such transformations.[96] These generic trumpings were designed to overwhelm the critical faculties of the French party, just as surely as the lavish feast, with its stately procession of courses, was designed to overawe their senses.

There is little here that would mark out *The Essex House Masque* as anything other than an official court masque, promoting royal policy to the court and its visiting ambassadors. But the masque was not only offered on behalf of the king to the French ambassador; it was also presented to the king by Doncaster. As a transaction between the courtier and his king, its substitution of Pallas for Hercules praises the king for his wisdom and abhorrence of violence. For despite Pallas's militarist and potentially subversive symbolic value, the manner of her victory requires no act of violence.[97] The masque thus locates itself firmly within the iconographic program of James's court, a program in which the king's association of himself with Pallas played a central symbolic role.[98] But in its introduction of the Worthies, the masque also registers Doncaster's commitment to the Protestant cause. This would have been obvious to those who recognized the masquers. One of the Holles boys was already in voluntary service in the Netherlands (and the Holles family were generally known as keen supporters of the cause), while Mountjoy Blount, another masquer, would shortly go there.[99] But the masque's advocacy of Doncaster's policies does not stop here. In its love-inspired transformation and its revels, the king is given a hint of the efficacy of a marriage as the means to achieve the royal goal of European peace. The masque declares that while wisdom may indeed conquer disorder, a fruitful peace can be realized only once the power of divine love has transformed the petrified Giants into men and they can mingle, in a dance of love, with the ladies of the court. Wisdom unaided offers only the sterility of bare rock. In the context of the French embassy, and given Doncaster's continued urging of a French match, the thrust of this point can hardly have been in doubt.

This emphasis on the need for love to supplement wisdom has domestic implications. The masque enacts the adage that "not stones but men make a state."[100] It attempts to allay the king's anxiety—especially acute in anticipation of the coming Parliament—over intrusions upon his prerogative from overambitious men who wished to subject the *arcana imperii* of foreign policy to their own vulgar scrutiny. These were matters only a divinely appointed monarch might legitimately contemplate.[101] It might be appropriate to read the masque in light of the recent *Proclamation against excesse of Lavish and Licentious Speech of matters of State*, with its insistence that the king's subjects avoid "excesse and presumption" and "containe themselves within that modest and reverent regard, of matters, above their reach and calling."[102] Perhaps the masque responds to the king's concern by presenting the petrifaction, through his wisdom, of the rebellious Giants, whose ambitions to meddle with celestial matters exceed their capacities?[103] If so, it goes beyond mere defensiveness, asserting that obedience comes through love. The figure of Prometheus—so often presented as a type of rebellion—is here, against expectation, transformed into a dutiful figure, subservient to the divine powers of the court. Having stolen the fire of heaven, he seeks divine approval for his act, and apparently gains it. The spectators cooperate in animating the rock, transforming vulgar rebels into Worthies—impeccable subjects, who will expend themselves in the service of their superiors (lines 184–86). Pallas conquered rebellion, but by destroying life she also removed the possibility of obedience. Men, not stones, make a state. It might not be entirely fanciful to associate Prometheus's resurrection of life from the stony punishment of Pallas with the king's summoning of a new Parliament; for what was Parliament other than a moribund body, petrified for its over-ambition by the king's wisdom, and now redeemed by his grace? The point would, once again, have been suggested for those who could identify the masquers, for the Holles boy who seems most likely to have danced in the masque was then seeking a parliamentary seat.[104]

While transactions such as these would have been accessible to many among the courtly spectators, a number of rather more intimate addresses might have been taking place. In its employment of a group of young gentlemen to demonstrate a transformation from rampant vice to refined manners through the divine love and wisdom emanating from the monarch, the masque may gesture toward the scheme for the "academy of honor" currently being promoted by Buckingham. There are clear general parallels between such a scheme and a masque depicting the transformation through the royal will of vicious young gentlemen into models of obedience and heroic virtue. But the parallels run closer: the masque appears to echo the symbolic vocabulary of the recent proposal. If the proposition does not reach the eyes of the king, notes one of Bolton's endorsers, it would be turned to stone: "like them that beeheld *Medusa*'s head." Its only hope, comments Bolton in his dedicatory epistle, lies in that "incomparable wisdome, and bountie, whose roial will, and powr are properly that celestial fire, which can quicken this *Promethian* clay."[105] Given the presence of both Buckingham and the king at Doncaster's entertainment, and given Doncaster's subsequent involvement in the Lords' committee on the matter, it is not entirely fanciful to imagine that the masque may have been part of the promotional campaign for the academy. Doncaster, in fact, enjoyed connections with several figures associated with the scheme. A list of proposed members dating from 1626 included, among 84 so-called "essentials," Doncaster's erstwhile secretary, Francis Nethersole, Ben Jonson, Inigo Jones, and Sir Robert Ayton.[106] The goals of the academy are communicated in the masque with a certain wry humor. In his claim that he will "manners so refine," Prometheus appears to offer a punning compliment to Buckingham for his recent marriage to Katherine Manners. The pun appears to allude to the objections of her family, who had questioned the couple's sexual virtue when, prior to the marriage's formal agreement, their daughter had spent a night in the house of Buckingham's mother.[107] Such a pun merges with the masque's emphasis on the virtuous conduct of courtship, and serves to locate it as a parallel to Van Dyck's *Continence of Scipio* in its celebration of the Buckingham—Manners marriage.

Although the masque bears witness to an alliance between Doncaster and Buckingham on certain domestic policies, it also suggests a degree of rivalry between them over, among other things, the conventions of masquing—a rivalry which involved a quest for the apt employment of French styles of court entertainment. In the masque sponsored by Buckingham the previous winter, a masque of giants had been proposed but not performed. Because the reason given for rejecting it was lack of space in the masquing room, the introduction of an antimasque of giants at Doncaster's residence in the following year looks rather like a piece of courtly one-upmanship.[108] Indeed, a number of parallels between the Buckingham masque and *The Essex House Masque* suggest a rather tense relationship between the two sponsors. Buckingham's masque had been a light, comic affair, performed by courtiers, which lacked the depth and dignity of a court masque.[109] It revolved around a discussion between a scholar and a Master of Revels over the appropriate ingredients of a masque, and it hinged upon the summoning, through the power of Orpheus, of a group of rebellious spirits, and their transformation into dutiful courtiers. The Buckingham masque incorporated an allusion—perhaps a little critical—to *Lord Hay's Masque*. The Master of Revels rejected the followers of Orpheus—those "Wooddes, Mountaines, and Wylde Beastes" which the scholar wished to introduce—on the grounds both of lack of space and of repetition: "for Mountaines this is but a small Roome; A Maske of Trees came in at my Lord Heyses Marriage."[110] It is hard to avoid the inference that the dancing beasts, trees, and mountains (the "mynes") which open *The Essex House Masque* are a direct response to their rejection in the Buckingham entertainment. Buckingham's masque had turned upon the transformation, through the removal of vizards, of a group of rebellious spirits into dutiful courtiers. If this entertainment was, in fact, the "running masque" of the previous season, it may well have been the arbitrary and ill-contrived character of this metamorphosis, with its lack of a coherent motivating fable, that occasioned the contemporary objections to it.[111] To this rather slipshod work, the carefully integrated double metamorphosis of *The Essex House Masque* may be seen as a corrective, demonstrating how the French fashion for transforming the masquers might be incorporated into the unifying fiction of an English masque. In its inconsequential character, Buckingham's entertainment may in fact be closer to the French *ballets* than Doncaster's, but it does not approach the aesthetic unity or philosophical weight of *The Essex House Masque*.

The politics of the masque are as much about rivalries between writers as they are concerned with competition between patrons. *The Essex House Masque* offers a political and literary corrective to the two recent masques that had addressed the question of England's response to the Bohemian crisis: the *Courtly Masque* of Middleton and Rowley, and Jonson's *Pan's Anniversary*. *The Essex House Masque* attempts to negotiate between the extreme positions represented by those works, presenting a case for responsible action in defense of the Protestant cause.

In *Pan's Anniversary*—a masque performed at court in front of both regular and extraordinary French ambassadors just two days earlier—Jonson had presented England as a golden world of pastoral *otium*, rudely invaded by a generically and politically inappropriate militarism.[112] Martin Butler has shown how Jonson used this generic conflict to explain the royal response to those Protestants who wished to see England offer military support to her beleaguered continental coreligionists.[113] According to Jonson, England was enjoying the "peace and pleasure" afforded by "*Great* Pan" (lines 255, 239–40), and had no need to trouble herself with foreign quarrels. The intruders who attempted to disturb her peace were therefore dismissed—transformed into sheep, allowing the shepherds to resume their rustic revelry. The seasonal delights of the court were not for long disrupted by foreign troubles. Small wonder that those with Protestant sympathies, like John Chamberlain, were offended by the masque's introduction of a puritan, "to be flowted and abused."[114]

Jonson grounded his defense of English isolationism on the authority of *The Kings Majesties Declaration to His Subjects Concerning lawfull Sports to be used* (London, 1618)—a tract demonstrating the legitimacy of "lawful recreations upon Sundays after evening prayers ended, and upon Holy-Days." Jonson ostentatiously appealed to the language of the *Declaration* to underpin his endorsement of rustic pursuits: *"This is the Shepherds Holy-day"* (lines 10, 24), the masque insisted, repeatedly. The appeal to the authority of the royal *Declaration* was a prudent move, but the presentation of England's isolation as a holiday raised at least as many questions as it answered. A Holy Day was a period of respite from work. With calls for English military intervention in Europe building to a crescendo, the advocacy of holiday festivity and careless leisure in *Pan's Anniversary* could appear tactless or untimely.

The intemperateness of Jonson's pastoral response did not go unnoticed. *The Essex House Masque* inverts Jonson's pastoral idyll by means of its first antimasque, in which Tellus summons her creatures to a revel in celebration of her anticipated defeat of the gods. Tellus's revel gestures toward the idyllic pastoral of *Pan's Anniversary* by its incorporation of such golden age topics as the harmonious coexistence of lion and lamb. While the grim lion and the sober sheep may here dance together, they do so in what is nonetheless an antimasque—a wild and discordant dance of beasts. This is a ghastly parody of *Pan's Anniversary*: nature here is no gilded Arcadia, presided over by the beneficent Pan; it is under the sway of Pan's antitype, the wild and passionate Tellus. Violent and uncouth, it is in need of redemption. This antipastoral redefinition of nature allows no space in which rustic pastimes might legitimately function. Tellus's rustic revel is not only discordant, it is also intemperate in both narrative and generic terms: it is a victory dance that precedes the victory it is supposed to celebrate, and an antimasque presenting itself as a "revel" (the stately, harmonious dance with which a masque conventionally concludes). The untimeliness of the leisure proposed in *Pan's Anniversary* is underlined by the masque's quotation of the very authorizing phrase from the royal *Declaration* on which Jonson had grounded his masque: "*This is the Shepherds Holy-day*" is perverted by Tellus into "For our revenge a hollyday" (line 34).

By thrusting into relief the intemperateness of Tellus's antipastoral revel, *The Essex House Masque* raises questions about the timeliness of Jonson's pastoral masque. Those with reasonably long memories might have noticed that, in criticizing *Pan's Anniversary* for its failure to reconcile revelry with responsibility, the masque articulates a position that Jonson himself had advanced three years earlier, in *Pleasure Reconciled to Virtue*—a position he had now betrayed. Indeed, the masque approaches the kind of explicit critique of Jonson's *Pleasure* that had appeared in Middleton's *Inner Temple Masque* of 1619.[115] And the transformations at the heart of the masque confirm the riposte to Jonson for his dismissal of the possibility of military intervention in Europe and his rejection of the heroic mode. Where *Pan's Anniversary* handled its militarist intruders with scorn, converting them into sheep, *The Essex House Masque* converts its earth-born creatures into the well-mannered military paragons who comprise its main masque.

By introducing the Nine Worthies *The Essex House Masque* returns explicitly to the heroic mode of Middleton's *Courtly Masque*; and yet it does so without reprising the strident tone that distinguished the *Courtly Masque*. Here is no clarion call to arms, no strident indictment of courtly pride and corruption; on the contrary, the Worthies are dissociated from the vulgar militancy of the earlier work: the achievement of a lasting peace is associated with them without the spelling out of any precise military implications. As such, *The Essex House Masque* manages to steer a course between the militant Protestantism of Middleton's *Courtly Masque* and the courtly pacifism of Jonson's *Pan's Anniversary*, without abandoning Doncaster's moderate and politic urging of action in regard to the Palatinate.

Consequences

The Essex House Masque manages to weave together in a remarkably coherent fashion a number of different, even competing, policy imperatives. It hints at both the desirability of a French marriage alliance and the possibility of English military intervention in defense of European Protestantism. It does so without explicitly undermining either James's pacifism, Louis's desire to suppress the Huguenots, or Spanish priority in the marriage stakes. This does not, however, mean it can be regarded as a diplomatic success. In the short term it may have had some effect in persuading Cadenet that he should urge his monarch to reach a peaceful settlement with the Huguenots; but Cadenet had barely left England with this policy in mind before a rapidly dispatched French mission to Madrid pulled off a settlement of the Valteline conflict, leaving Louis free to turn on the Huguenots.[116] As Edward Herbert, the English ambassador in Paris, noted in a letter to Buckingham of 15 February 1621, the question was no longer "whether a warre shall be made, but where, when, and how."[117]

From the king's point of view the more important auditors were not the French but the Spanish. The masque needed to persuade them of his resolve with regard to the Palatinate and of the seriousness of his interest in the French proposal. While one or two minor intelligencers may have been thrown into a momentary flutter by the English reception of the embassy and the Spanish ambassador himself "not a litle injealoused" at Cadenet's reception, the wily Gondomar was not fooled for long. He soon reasserted his authority by forcing the king to reprimand or dismiss various loyal servants whom he deemed too sympathetic to French interests: Doncaster was scolded, and Sir Robert Naunton was accused of raising the specter of a French marriage and was hurriedly dismissed—despite the fact that he had been operating under the king's instructions.[118]

Perhaps the most incisive contemporary comment on the evening was that of Girolamo Lando, the Venetian ambassador. Having noted the enormous expense of the entertainment, Lando concluded that, "whereas the French ambassador has enjoyed these airy demonstrations, the Spaniard has what is more solid and important, being more influential then ever over his Majesty or over those who guide him, making use for his own advantage of festivities, masques and all distractions from business."[119] The French themselves soon realized the true state of affairs. Ambassador Tillières noted in his *Mémoires* that the English plan had all along been "de contenter l'Espagne en choses solides, voulait satisfaire notre légereté avec des apparences sans fruit."[120]

Just as the masque achieved little or nothing for the king, so it was an expensive diplomatic disaster for Doncaster: it achieved none of his goals, and only served to confirm his already unrivaled position as a host of entertainments of unparalleled extravagance. Indeed, the evening's entertainment was regarded as so stunning that it became, for a time, the standard by which such receptions were judged.[121] As soon as the embassy departed, the king reverted to his pro-Spanish policy, and no serious intervention on behalf of the Palatinate was forthcoming. Prophetic hopes of the Parliament of 1621 were not realized. It did not, like the reformed antimasquers, keep "within the compass of dutifull subjects," and the king quickly tired of its intrusive, demanding, and uncooperative spirit, and dissolved it within the year.[122] Even the noble academy, despite being an idea that genuinely appealed to James, was never formally instituted.[123] One might, of course, feel that Doncaster had the last laugh; for a French marriage was eventually arranged, and Doncaster was instrumental in negotiating it; but that was years later, and under dramatically changed circumstances—circumstances that Doncaster and his masque had no effect in bringing about. Perhaps the most appropriate judgment on the success of the masque is to note the fact that Doncaster seems never to have sponsored another one.

Finally, the literary politics in which the masque was engaged had their influence, which we may trace in Ben Jonson's royal entertainment of the following summer, *The Gypsies Metamorphosed.* One of the obstacles to our understanding of that entertainment is the lack of any clear sense of why the gypsies change. Not only does the metamorphosis fail to grow naturally and inevitably out of the action of the masque, but Jonson is at pains to point up its arbitrariness and inexplicability. In an epilogue added to the printed text he drew attention to the problem, suggesting that his own inadequacies were to blame:

> You have beheld (and with delight) theire change,
> And how they came transformd may thinck it strange,
> It being a thing not touched at by our *Poet;*
> Good *Ben* slept there, or else forgot to showe it.[124]

Critics have been understandably reluctant to take such a statement at face value, not least because in this work above all others the poet seems so supremely in command of his material, so keenly aware of what he is about.[125] If we pause to reconsider the problem in the light of both *The Essex House Masque* and the recently discovered masque text emanating from the Buckingham circle in this period, two things become clear. First, there was at this time an outburst of privately sponsored masquing among leading courtiers (probably as a result of the king's financial difficulties)—an outburst that threatened, or appeared to threaten, Jonson's preeminence as a deviser of court masques. Jonson was scoffed at in the anonymous masque uncovered by James Knowles, and sniped at in *The Essex House Masque.* Second, these new masques were obsessed with the idea of metamorphosis: the text discovered by Knowles turns upon a metamorphosis of spirits into courtiers, and *The Essex House Masque* features no less than two transformations. We know that when Jonson felt threatened by rival writers or unwelcome developments in masquing he habitually incorporated critiques or parodies of them into his masques. We think of Vangoose and his ludicrous antimasques in *The Masque of Augurs*; of Jonson's mockery of Jones in *Love's Welcome at Bolsover*; of his parody of Campion in *The Irish Masque at Court*; or, indeed, of his response to Robert White's *Cupid's Banishment* in *Pleasure Reconciled to Virtue*.[126] In the light of this practice, it seems reasonable to suggest that the arbitrary metamorphosis of the gypsies and Jonson's comic self-deprecation about it should be interpreted as a parody of current masque fashions. *The Gypsies Metamorphosed* was Jonson's attempt to brush aside his rivals and reassert his own preeminence in the masque. While he may, in the short term, have lost the commissions for Buckingham's extravaganzas of 1623 and 1624 to John Maynard, if we contemplate the erasure of his rivals from the received history of the masque, and the oblivion from which *The Essex House Masque* has only now emerged, we must conclude that, in the long run, he did rather a good job.[127]

THREE

ॐ

Scenes and Costumes

A masque presented in a private residence at an individual's expense may reasonably be presumed to have lacked the full financial and spatial resources of a court masque at Whitehall. This might be thought to imply restrictions on the scale and magnificence of scenery and costuming. The use of a traverse and standing scenes, together with decorated doorways for entrances and exits, appears to have been the norm for private house entertainments.[1] For *Lovers Made Men*, presented at the Wardrobe four years earlier, Nicholas Lanier had designed such a scene (probably a traverse with entries) behind an elaborate triumphal arch: it featured a raised bank and a grove of myrtles presented in perspective.[2] But we should not leap too quickly to the presumption that *The Essex House Masque* was a minimal affair. Doncaster brooked no expense in enhancing the magnificence of the feast that accompanied the masque, and it is impossible to imagine him scrimping on the costuming of his performers. Our inferences about the staging of the masque must be based on a careful examination of its text.

The masquing space available in the Great Gallery at Essex

House appears to have been restricted. A narrow and shallow stage, perhaps measuring in the teens, seems a reasonable inference, both from our knowledge of the layout of the gallery in the early seventeenth century (figure 16, and above, pages 77–80), and from the small number of performers who took part in the masque. The scenic requirements of the masque, moreover, place more pressure on height than on breadth. The masque requires very few performers. In addition to the nine masquers who doubled up as the second antimasquers, two speaking roles are called for (Pallas and Prometheus), and at least seven dancers for the first antimasque, if only one representative of each of the several creatures summoned forth by Tellus appears (Tree, Mine, Lion, Ape, Sheep, Boar, and Stag). If Tellus herself does not appear (and there is no reason to think from her song that she does), the singer may have doubled as Pallas in the next antimasque, thus reducing the number of performers still further, to a minimum of 18—a potentially significant number, in light of Doncaster's preference for the number nine and its multiples.

Much may be inferred about the appearance of the performers themselves by a consideration of contemporary masques and emblems; for the characters of the masque were all, by and large, conventional figures. Although the voice of Tellus summons the first antimasque, there is no indication that she herself appeared: the opening song is *"supposed to be don by the earth,"* and its first words identify its source for the auditors: "The glad Earth summons to appeare." The figure of Earth did, however, have a number of conventional attributes, such as a garment of fruits and flowers and a globe.[3] The other speakers, Pallas and Prometheus, would have been readily recognizable. Pallas was invariably depicted helmeted, armed, and bearing a shield or cuirass with the Gorgon's head on it (see, for example, figure 7, and Inigo Jones's sketch for a statue from this period, figure 6).[4] Prometheus was recognizable by his stolen fire, traditionally carried in a fennel stalk: an image to which Jones had earlier alluded in *The Lords' Masque* (figure 9).

The identification of the first antimasquers would have been assisted by Tellus's song, in which the revelers are carefully enumerated: a tree, mines, a lion, an ape, a sheep, a boar, and a stag. Jones had employed dancing trees in *Lord Hay's Masque*, though there are no surviving sketches of them. His sketches for a lion and an ape for the antimasque of *Tempe Restored* (1632) give us some idea of their likely appearance in *The Essex House Masque* (figures 3, 4). The presence among his drawings of an unidentified design for animal-headed antimasquers that Orgel and Strong assign to a period around 1620 offers a tempting prospect (figure 5).[5] Might these male and female figures be a couple of "sober sheepe" from Tellus's revel? They would certainly suit such roles. However, the recent demonstration by Martin Butler that other sketches from this period were probably associated with *Pan's Anniversary* should give us pause: *Pan's Anniversary* featured the transformation of antimasquers into sheep.

"The mynes of mocion must pertake | Which neyther growth nor earthquake make" (lines 27–28). What exactly were the mines summoned by Tellus, and how might they have moved? That Tellus means by "mynes" something other than repositories of mineral wealth is apparent both from her own denial that this motion will produce growth (the means by which minerals were thought to be generated), and by the lack of any reference to precious metals in the masque; it is not simply a rehash of *The Memorable Masque*, which had focused upon the fabled gold mines of Virginia.[6] In fact, Tellus uses the term "mynes" in the unusual sense of "subterranean cavities" (*OED*, *sb*. 1.d). What we seem to have here is an attempt to prepare the audience for the revelation of the cave at the end of the first antimasque. But what motion, exactly, was involved? There are two obvious possibilities. Either the whole scene depicting the rocky mount containing the cave moved (this seems excessive and confusing), or the motion was suggested by an actor hidden in a rock-shaped machine moving away from the mountain scene. Jones had earlier employed the conceit of a rock breaking away from a mined mountain in *The Memorable Masque* (lines 150–54).[7] And dancing rocks had been suggested in the French *Ballet des Argonautes* (1614) by devices made of painted gauze stretched over wooden frames.[8] This seems the most plausible explanation for the action.

The young gentlemen who danced as Giants in the second antimasque were not, as far as we know, renowned for their extraordinary height, and since they were not expressly introduced as Giants, they must have been readily identifiable as such. This identification may in part have been effected by their contrast either with some very short torchbearers or an unusually diminutive mountain scene; certain physical features would no doubt have been emphasized. The Giants were traditionally represented as figures of terrible, troll-like aspect: half-naked, bearded, and equipped with clubs or rocks.[9] Such attributes are not features of other contemporary giants in masques, who tend to be presented as absurd, burlesque figures.[10] Their reappearance—again without explicit identification—as the Worthies might be thought to present problems, were it not for the conventional association of the number nine with the Worthies, and for the recent fashion for depicting the Worthies in masques. The conceit had been used in at least two entertainments of the period: Middleton's *Inner Temple Masque* of 1619, and his and Rowley's *Courtly Masque* (1619–20). Although no sketches for these figures survive, other contemporary evidence suggests that they were conventionally represented as armed, helmeted figures with only the most perfunctory rendering of temporal and cultural distinctions.[11] Such distinctions tended to be made, if at all, by lances bearing pennons depicting the badge of each worthy (figure 10); such devices may (if they were employed at all) have been carried by the torchbearers.[12] In this light, one wonders whether Jones's drawing of an heroic statue, perhaps associated with his scene for a "Pallace of Perfection," might have pertained to *The Essex House Masque* (figure 11). Such statues might have been used in the discovery scene to suggest the stony forms from which the Worthies were to be animated. It is perhaps more likely, however, that the masquers themselves would have been discovered in statue-like poses prior to their animation: this would make good theatrical sense (as is witnessed by the climactic scene in *The Winter's Tale*), and would square with the animation of statues in *The Lords' Masque*.

While the probable appearance of the performers may be determined with some certainty, the staging of the masque is more difficult to reconstruct. This is because the text does not offer the ample descriptions characteristic of retrospective accounts. It does, however, allow us to make a number of inferences about the scenes and machines employed in the performance. At least two scenic devices are demanded by the stage directions: a cave that may be hidden and revealed, from which the second antimasque might issue, and something resembling a mount for the antimasquers to ascend in their assault on the heavens, where they might assume fixed places. Several other devices are implied by the text of the masque. First, the Giants' assault on the stars and Pallas's subsequent recalling of them to their proper places would have been redundant were it not accompanied by some visual suggestion, if not an actual representation, of the disruption and restoration of the heavens. Second, Pallas's "locking up" of the Giants and Prometheus's subsequent liberation of them from their rocky prisons implies that two scenic transformations were represented. At least three changes of scene thus appear to be required in the masque: the discovery of a cave, the enclosure of the antimasquers in earth, and their revelation as the masquers. How were such changes most likely to have been effected?

The first antimasque demanded little by way of scenery. First, it required an entrance or entrances from which Tellus's creatures may be "*calld out by the songe.*" These antimasquers are not, like those of the second, summoned from earth; they are said merely to be "*calld out*" by Tellus, who refers to her creatures not as a new birth, but as young children: "those whom she doth foster heare" (line 22). Her creatures need not, therefore, have emerged as newborns from the earth itself, but could have entered from the side of the scene. Second, it required a backdrop in front of which the dancers might disport themselves. A simple painted traverse would have served here, but, given what follows, a more substantial fixed scene or machine would also have been appropriate.[13] As a setting for a dance of animals, trees, and mines, a sylvan scene, incorporating a rocky or mountainous aspect, like that of *Oberon*, would have been appropriate. It would afford a context for the dancing trees and mines, and would form a bridge to the second antimasque, which begins with the discovery of a cave.[14] Of some interest in this respect is an unassigned sketch for a back shutter for such a scene by Inigo Jones, which Orgel and Strong date to the period 1619–23 (figure 22).[15] This incorporates the sylvan setting, the prominent trees, and the mountains we would expect to find in such a scene. One wonders, however, whether the mountains are as prominent as they would have to be to allow for the appearance of the cave. One wonders also whether a back shutter, with its suggestion of a full proscenium and possibly perspective stage, would not have exceeded the fairly minimal requirements for the first antimasque, which seems to require only a painted traverse.

At the close of the first antimasque, the revelers are said to "*vanish,*" at which point, we are informed, "*the cave appeares, from whence issue .9. giants the supposed sonnes and champions of the earth*" (lines 36–38). From that cave issues the second antimasque. The cave seems most likely to have been a simple entryway, an opening in the scene large enough to

Figure 22   Inigo Jones, Shutter for a landscape (*c.* 1619–23).
Reproduced by permission of the Chatsworth Settlement Trustees.

allow the Giants to enter the performing space. This is all that is required for the antimasque; there·is no call for the elaborate interior of *Oberon*, in which the masquers were discovered.[16] Since the Giants first dance and then ascend the scene, the cave entrance must have been on the lowest part of the scene: either at stage or at floor level. The discovery of the cave might have come as the direct consequence of the movement of the mine away from the mountain in the first antimasque, obviating the need for a separate scene, painted on a traverse, for the first antimasque. But since some sort of curtain must have hidden the scene from the spectators before the start of the masque, a painted traverse, dropped after the first antimasque, would have been appropriate.

At the end of their dance, having announced their assault on the stars, the Giants *"fall of by degrees, and clime to theire places, where settlinge themselves Pallas enters, and veiwinge them* [exclaims] | *Thus I locke up your madnesse"* (lines 85–88). This direction implies a succession of actions: first, the Giants ascend the scenery and settle themselves in a number of prearranged locations; then, when Pallas appears, they turn to stone. What exactly is entailed here? That some sort of re-entry of earth took place is clear from Pallas's comment that she is "returninge Earth her one"; yet the logic of the action and the stage directions suggest something slightly different from a simple return to the cave. The logic of the action—an assault on the heavens—and the stage directions—*"clime to theire places"*—require that the Giants leave the dance floor and ascend the scene. What this suggests is that the cave must have been topped by a mount—a mount equipped, moreover, with "greces," or steps, for ascent and descent (as in *The Memorable Masque*, lines 115–19), and perhaps with niches for the performers to enter and settle themselves prior to their petrifaction, such as had appeared in a number of Italian *intermedi* and French *ballets*.[17] Although a painted shutter of a mount and cave, as in *Oberon* (figure 23), would have done the trick,

Figure 23　Inigo Jones, Design for a *machina versatilis* for
Oberon (1611): Scene of Rocks. Reproduced by permission
of the Chatsworth Settlement Trustees.

this would have been unnecessarily elaborate; all that is really required is a freestanding scene depicting a mount with cave below. The latter was a traditional pageant device, regularly employed in early masques and private house entertainments (figure 24), and would have been adequate for the demands of the action (the Giants' ascent of the scene: a vertical movement) and easy to accommodate in a narrow chamber.[18]

Pallas's exclamation, "Thus I locke up your madnesse," may simply comment on their petrifaction, but the verb perhaps suggests imprisonment within something, rather than just a conversion of substance. The discovery scene that later reveals the main masque, with its animation of human life from the stone, demands that the masquers be made once more visible to the audience. Prometheus's speech, with its direct reference to the petrified Giants in the phrase "this stony judgment," might be thought to imply that they remain visible throughout, but all it actually requires is the continued visibility of the stone into which they have been converted. The transformation song portrays the masquers as stone (line 214), and does not allude to them as men until its third and final stanza, at which point (and not before) the main masque is discovered: "Then view the spring of man begun | By your one sun" (lines 208–09). The disappearance of the performers is, moreover, a crucial piece of stagecraft, allowing them to change into their masque costumes while Prometheus delivers his speech.

The most obvious means of petrifying of the masquers would have been the *machina versatilis*—a double-faced device turned by an engine beneath the stage.[19] One side could have depicted a mount (with cave below) featuring concaves within which the masquers might position themselves; on turning it could then have presented a mere rock face or bare mountainside. The revelation of the main masque could then have been achieved by another turn of the machine, revealing the masquers in their fresh costumes, frozen in tableau but

Figure 24   Inigo Jones, Design for a cave and mount. Reproduced
by permission of the Chatsworth Settlement Trustees.

slowly coming to life, and ready to make their descent to the dancing space. The gradual animation of the petrified masquers is a crucial piece of stagecraft, allowing for the kind of eye-catching movement recommended by Lord Bacon, who urged in his essay "Of Masques and Triumphs," that "the Masquers, or any other, that are to come down from the *Scene,* have some Motions, upon the *Scene* it selfe, before their Comming down: For it drawes the Eye strangely, and makes it with great pleasure, to desire to see that, it cannot perfectly discerne."[20]

The locking up and revelation of the Giants might, of course, have been achieved by other means. The masquers might have disposed themselves on a fixed scenic mount in places where rock-shaped machines would be raised to hide them individually—a method described in the stagecraft manual of Nicola Sabbattini.[21] This technique had been employed (disastrously, as it turned out) in *Lord Hay's Masque,* in which a series of individual trees were supposed to hide and then reveal the masquers, but which had, in the event, failed to do so.[22] An alternative method would have been to enclose the entire scene by means of a *machina ductilis,* or moving shutter system, as in *Oberon.* But the *machina ductilis* seems unnecessarily elaborate for the scenic requirements of the masque.

Two further requirements need explanation: the moving of the stars, and the entrances and exits for the first antimasquers, for Pallas, and for Prometheus. The disordering of the stars accompanying the rebellion of the Giants and Pallas's restoration of their order reads like a cue for an ingenious "transposition of lights." It suggests a horizontally divided scene. The cave and mount might have been surmounted by a depiction of the heavens, along the lines of the device deployed by Jones in *The Lords' Masque* of 1613, in which eight stars were displayed, moving *"in an exceeding strange and delightfull maner."*[23] Alternatively, a disruption of the lighting in the chamber could have created a similar effect more simply. Finally, performers other than the nine masquers might easily have made their entries and exits through a doorway in the chamber itself.

The *Essex House Masque* appears, in all likelihood, to have been fairly straightforward in its staging and its scenery. Its designers appear to have conceived of the stage primarily in old-fashioned, symbolic terms. The masque required a performing area with several entrances, a traverse, and a standing scene of two or three levels (cave, mount, and possibly heavens). It featured three scene changes: the revelation of the cave, the locking up of the Giants, and the discovery of the main masque. These effects could have been achieved by a simple, freestanding *machina versatilis*. As such, the masque could easily have been staged within the confines of a gallery in a private residence, even were it less ample than the one in Essex House appears to have been.

FOUR

ॐ

Design, Invention, and Authorship

The production of a masque involved several levels of creation. First came the act of invention, which was, as D. J. Gordon reminded us, the discovery of a motivating idea, fable, or argument.[1] The construction of a governing design or structure and a text to adumbrate the argument came later. In weighing up the evidence for attributing *The Essex House Masque*, it is worth keeping such distinctions in mind. Although we can probably discern the taste of the sponsor in the masque's transformation of the antimasquers into masquers, the working out of a fable to motivate that transformation was no doubt left to the discretion of the inventor or inventors.[2] Although the production of a masque was a collaborative process, involving designers, poets, painters, choreographers, musicians, and performers, the invention of a fable tended to be the province of the designer or the poet, or of them both. Either one of them may have received the initial commission to prepare the entertainment: while the poet was perhaps traditionally the master of ceremonies, by the early seventeenth century the designer increasingly tended to usurp that role.[3] We might seek clarification about Hay's habits in commissioning masques by considering the production of *Lovers Made Men* in 1617. The quarto text, printed to accompany the performance, makes no mention of the relative responsibilities of poet or designer; the folio text of 1640, however, implicitly presents the masque as Jonson's own, in its generous yet restricting acknowledgment of the role played by Nicholas Lanier, "*who ordered and made both the Scene, and the Musicke.*"[4] Jonson's touchiness about matters of precedence in the wake of his disastrous quarrel with Inigo Jones makes one a little reluctant to take such retrospective protestations at face value. Nor does the poet's claim to priority here necessarily imply that he first received the commission for the masque. Hay's household had close contacts with court musicians (Gaultier the lutenist, for example); the commission may well have been handed to Lanier in the first instance. In sum, we cannot be certain how the commission for *The Essex House Masque* would have reached its inventors.

Design and Invention

A number of parallels between the scenes and costumes required by *The Essex House Masque* and those of the court masques raise the possibility that Inigo Jones might have been its designer.[5] Many of these parallels no doubt derive from the common stock of mythological material from which masques were generally constructed. Dancing rocks and trees, the beastly revel, the figures of Pallas, Prometheus, and the Worthies—all were fairly common topics in contemporary entertainments. But a number of parallels are more distinctive than the deployment of standard mythological *topoi*, and several of them point to consistencies between the underlying argument or invention of this masque and those of others with which Jones was involved.

Three areas of congruence deserve our attention. First, there is the striking association of Prometheus and the ancient heroes or, more specifically, with the Nine Worthies. This appears in *The Lords' Masque* and again in *The Essex House Masque*. In both masques Prometheus is responsible for the reanimation of petrified stones or statues. That the animation of stones or statues was at least in part a distinctively Jonesian conceit, and not merely an idea attributable to Campion, is confirmed by the fact that Jones returned to it once more in *Albion's Triumph* (1632), a masque he invented together with Aurelian Townshend in 1632.[6] There is another revealing parallel here: the scene for *Albion's Triumph* featured the Gorgons' heads from the very frieze that had been so topical at the time of *The Essex House Masque*.[7] Second, there is a general similarity between the fable of *The Essex House Masque* and that of *Tempe Restored* (1632)—another masque designed and invented by Jones, the verses for which were prepared by Townshend. The fable for *Tempe Restored* was borrowed from the *Balet Comique* of Beaujoyeulx; it featured the triumph of Pallas over Circe, and the retransformation of the latter's beastly lovers into men. A third and final point of congruence between *The Essex House Masque* and the work of Jones is the visual conceit of Pallas's imprisonment of the Giants in a rocky outcrop. Some eight or nine years later Jones would employ a similar device for a play at Somerset House in which Pallas appeared in "a Whight Cloude which turnes to a roke" (the sketch for the scene shows Pallas descending in a cloud machine).[8] Without being in any way dispositive, such parallels are certainly suggestive.

The regular return to favored devices suggested by the preceding account squares with contemporary accounts of Jones's working practices. In his notorious "Expostulation" with Jones (*c.* 1631), Jonson accused the architect of a kind of weary self-plagiarism:

> who can reflect
> On the new priming of thy old Signe postes
> Reviving with fresh coulors the pale Ghosts
> Of thy dead Standards: or (with miracle) see
> Thy twice conceyvd, thrice payd for Imagery?[9]

Jonson here complains not so much about the redeployment of actual painted properties (these were usually demolished in fits of gleeful destruction by the spectators) as about the reemployment of ideas and conceptions. There is, however, surprisingly little evidence for the kind of widespread rehashing here implied. Herford and Simpson draw attention to the variant designs for *Oberon* (the earliest of which were apparently unused), and Ian Donaldson points to the reemployment of material from the unperformed *Neptune's Triumph* in *The Fortunate Islands*, noting that Jonson himself was equally culpable on this particular occasion.[10] This hardly amounts to an overwhelming case against the architect. The parallels and continuities we have noticed between Jones's work and *The Essex House Masque* may provide confirmation of the kind of self-plagiarism decried by Jonson.

That *The Essex House Masque* might provide a gloss on Jonson's remarks in the "Expostulation" may possibly be confirmed by an aside the poet tossed out a few lines after the passage quoted above. "What story shall," inquires Jonson, "Of all the Worthyes hope t'outlast thy one"?[11] The primary meaning of the question is, of course, that Jones knows only one story, which, like those of the Worthies, will be eternally reiterated. But might it not also involve a wicked play on the identity of that tale? Jonson is, after all, fairly precise in his charges against Jones: "What story of the Worthies will outlast *yours*?" Although the prominence of the Nine Worthies in

The Essex House Masque is not paralleled in other known masques of Jones, the revelation of clusters of "Worthies," or ancient heroes, was a recurring conceit. It appeared, for instance, in *Albion's Triumph* (1632), in *Coelum Britannicum* (1634), and also in an unidentified masque, possibly dating from 1619, featuring a "Pallace of Perfection" adorned with statues of such figures.[12]

The possibility that Jonson's "Expostulation" involved a direct attack on Jones's employment of the Worthies in *The Essex House Masque* squares with the evidence, noticed in an earlier chapter, that the masque was devised by someone who was intimately familiar with Jonson's masques and not entirely sympathetic to the poet. And the explicit reference in its first antimasque to *Pan's Anniversary*, performed a mere two days earlier, implies the involvement in the Essex House production of someone who was acquainted with the text of Jonson's masque prior to its performance. (*The Essex House Masque* could not, surely, have been invented, designed, and executed in a mere two days? The slightly unintegrated character of the first antimasque might, however, suggest that it was an afterthought to the main invention.) Aside from the poet himself, Jones, as the designer of *Pan's Anniversary*, is the most likely source of such a text. We might therefore wonder whether *The Essex House Masque* did not form an early step in the breakdown of relations between the poet and the designer.[13]

Although there is no firm evidence to connect Jones with *The Essex House Masque*, the available internal evidence points in his direction. Both the fable of the masque and the machinery employed to embody it have a decidedly Jonesian flavor. Against this subjective and therefore arguable impression must be set three points.[14] First, none of Jones's surviving designs may with certainty be associated with this masque. Second, the rather old-fashioned, emblematic staging implied by the text of the masque does not seem to square with Jones's move toward increasingly sophisticated landscape settings in the court masque.[15] And finally, no evidence allows us to discount the involvement of other designers, such as Nicholas Lanier, who had earlier worked for Doncaster.

Although we lack firm evidence to identify the designer, it is possible that we know who was responsible for executing his designs. A schedule of Doncaster's creditors, prepared some years after his death, survives in the House of Lords Record Office.[16] Among the late earl's creditors was one Mary Buckett, executor (and presumably widow) to Rowland Buckett, to whom £179 was owed. Rowland Buckett was a prominent Painter-Stainer who had worked, to great acclaim, as artificer or painter on triumphal arches for King James's accession, and on Lord Mayors' Shows under Anthony Munday in 1614 and Thomas Middleton in 1617.[17] Buckett was well known to aristocratic patrons: he worked on an entertainment for Robert Cecil, earl of Salisbury, at Hatfield House in 1612, and painted the earl of Rutland's tilting furniture in 1620.[18] We do not, however, know the nature of his work for Doncaster.

Authorship

Doncaster entertained on the most lavish scale, in a manner designed to overwhelm. For his entertainment of a French ambassador in 1617, he had commissioned a text from Jonson, the design and music from Nicholas Lanier—the premier poet and one of the leading musicians then working on the court masque. When he wanted, in 1621, to entertain another visiting French ambassador, he would surely have required a poet of similar caliber, even if he did not oversee the hiring himself. If not Jonson, then someone with comparable credentials.[19]

Was Jonson the author of the masque? With its weight of classical learning, its moral seriousness, and its emphasis on the transformative power of art, the masque features a number of recurrent Jonsonian preoccupations. Its Prometheus is modeled on the Daedalus of *Pleasure Reconciled to Virtue*, and its conflict between Pallas and the Giants owes much to that of Pallas and the Iron Age in *The Golden Age Restored*. The masque might even be said, in structural terms, to have grafted the transformation of *Lovers Made Men* onto that of *The Golden Age Restored*. And yet such similarities might equally well be assigned to a serious student of Jonson as to the master himself. Indeed, there are compelling reasons why the masque is unlikely to be Jonson's. First, there is orthographic evidence: the unusual spelling "ante-," in contrast to Jonson's favoured "antimasque." Second, there is the evidence presented in chapter 2 above, that *The Essex House Masque* incorporates an attack on *Pan's Anniversary*. And finally, there is the occasional obscurity or downright ineptness of the verse.

The masque is notable for the elegance of its songs and the smooth flow of its speeches—an elegance enhanced by its habitual use of enjambment. The logical and grammatical movement of lines is typically played off against the divisions of the verse (line ending, couplet, and caesura) to yield an overspill that plays against, without erasing, the bounds of the couplet. A clause will typically begin with a mid-line caesura; its completion will be implied by the line end or couplet close; but it will be modified by an additional clause. At its best this technique aptly registers the contours of a voice in conversation, as in Prometheus's gracious address to the royal audience:

> But the life I give
> shall weare in servinge you by whom⌃ I live
> Divinest powers.

> (lines 184–86)

A little unctuous in tone, perhaps, but an effective use of enjambment. Although enjambment is one of the more effective metrical devices of the masque, it is overused. It appears in almost every line, often without regard to the achievement of particular semantic effects (of the sixteen lines of the opening "Argument," all but lines 11 and 13 are enjambed). A further deficiency in the verse is its occasional unevenness—the result of hurried or careless composition. Consider, for instance, the following tortured antithesis, in which a Giant asserts that he and his fellows will "Binde truth apprentise, till to bee vertuous I Bee held a greater guilt then to bee us" (lines 72–73). It would be charitable to attribute this to an attempt to reflect the logical disorder of the Giants' actions. It might be possible to do so, were it not for the fact that a similar instance of such carelessness appears in Pallas's speech: "or thought these that the skarrs I Disabled heaven had in the former warres" (lines 94–95). This couplet represents an attempt to ask whether the Giants thought the gods were disabled by the scars incurred in the earlier wars. Such examples reveal a failure of the poet to engage in a thorough and careful polishing of his text. The versification of the masque thus reveals a considerable poetic talent at work, but not, perhaps, a fully controlled one. On balance, a craftsman of Jonson's caliber and perfectionist tendencies is unlikely to have been the author of such verse.

But who, other than Jonson, might have provided a masque for Doncaster in the winter of 1620–21? On the basis of the surviving text we may say with some certainty that its poet was a sedulous student of the court masque as practised by Jonson, Jones, and Campion; that he was able to respond with success to Doncaster's desire for French-style transformations in masques; that he was an intellectually ambitious poet, adept at handling the enjambed couplet, but not always careful in the polishing of his verse; and that he must have been in London in the winter of 1620. We might also conjecture that he was known as an accomplished writer of entertainments for the court and, furthermore, speculate that, if my assignation of the design and invention of the masque to Jones is correct, imagine that he was known to the architect. Who could lay claim to such credentials? Of those writers we now know, Daniel and Campion were dead, and Townshend was untried. Thomas Carew was a distant relative of Doncaster, and may have been known to him as the author of a country house entertainment for the Crofts family. Carew was adept at handling the enjambed couplet, and a tentative case can be made for his involvement.[20] But Carew had not, by this stage, established a reputation as a poet; nor had he written a court masque. Thomas Middleton, whose recent masques seem thematically proximate to *The Essex House Masque* might also be a feasible candidate; but, as I have argued elsewhere, orthographic evidence points away from his involvement.[21] Our attempt to identify a candidate among masque writers of repute in the winter of 1620 is aided by Ben Jonson's remark to William Drummond of the previous year, "That next himself only Fletcher and Chapman could make a Mask."[22] No masques by John Fletcher are now known; but George Chapman closely matches the profile of the author sketched above. He had longstanding experience of the court masque, having collaborated with Jones on *The Memorable Masque* in celebration of the marriage of Princess Elizabeth to the Elector Frederick—a masque performed for the royal family at Whitehall in 1613. He may also have written the *Masque of the Four Seasons*: a work recently identified by Martin Butler as the lost Christmas court masque of 1619.[23]

The Essex House Masque is striking for its careful, Jonsonian structuring, its sophisticated manipulation of classical myth interpreted in the light of neoplatonic philosophy, its revolution around the topos of metamorphosis, and its focus on the power of the Promethean artist. These attributes alone might tempt one to posit the involvement of Chapman. Who else, one wonders, might have pulled off the masque's triumphant merging of the Gigantomachy with the myth of Prometheus's creation of man? Chapman's interest in Prometheus was intense and of long standing.[24] He employed the figure of the

Promethean poet in his early "Hymnus in Noctem" (1594) and returned to it in a dedicatory poem for *The Iliads*, where he alluded to the Promethean faculty as one that "Can create men, and make even death to live."[25] Prometheus the aspiring Titan underlies the character of his greatest hero, Bussy D'Ambois; and Prometheus the thief of divine knowledge figured in a footnote to his translation of Hesiod's *Works and Days, The Georgicks of Hesiod* (1618).[26] What other writer so nearly approached a Jonsonian understanding of the masque? Such understanding informs the philosophical and dramatic antithesis of masque to antimasque, and its use of precisely four songs. Stephen Orgel cites Chapman as the sole exception to his dictum that Milton was "the only contemporary masque writer to conceive of the form in Jonsonian terms."[27] And Willa McClung Evans notes that "Chapman, more than any other writer, arranged his songs in the fashion of Jonson."[28] Typical also of Chapman is the use of two antimasques.[29] Topical parallels between Chapman's works and *The Essex House Masque* also abound. The structural and philosophical opposition between the civilizing order of Prometheus and the rustic revelry of Tellus is similar in form and function to the opposition established in the "Hymnus in Noctem" between true, Promethean poetry and the "Rude rurall dances" of false art.[30] Like all of Chapman's works, the masque displays an astonishing level of meteorological, astrological, and numerological precision.[31] We see this in the masque's allusion to "The lusting lookes of Venus, by which shee | Intreated Mars first to Adultery" (lines 164–65)—a reference that parallels the detailed account of the operation of Venus on Mars offered by Chapman in *Andromeda Liberata* (lines 305–20). The masque, moreover, appears to share with Chapman's continuation of Marlowe's *Hero and Leander* a commitment to the novel and unusual view that comets were celestial rather than terrestrial phenomena.[32] Finally, Chapman's interest in and knowledge of contemporary French history and literature are well evidenced by his plays on French themes: *Bussy D'Ambois*, the *Byron* plays, *Chabot, Admiral of France*. The masque would be quite at home in the Chapman canon. But not until we examine its style, orthography, and lexical composition does substantive evidence for Chapman's authorship emerge.

One of the stylistic strengths of the masque is, as noted above, its unusually adept and frequent use of the enjambed couplet. This was a form in which Chapman excelled: he had worked extensively in it, in his Homeric translations and his original verse. In Donald Foster's survey of elegiac verse of the period 1608–13, Chapman emerges as one of the more frequent users of enjambment at a rate, on Foster's count, of 36.6%.[33] The rate of enjambment exhibited in the masque (in its 136 pentameter lines) is considerably higher than this, at 62%.[34] This difference does not provide evidence against Chapman's authorship because enjambment rates appear to have risen in general during the early part of the century, and because they tended to rise in individual poets, as they gained in confidence and skill. Thus, Foster shows Shakespeare moving from a rate of 9% in *The Comedy of Errors* to a rate of 46.5% in *The Winter's Tale*.[35] Perhaps a better point of comparison might be Chapman's later poem *Pro Vere, Autumni Lachrymae* (1622), which exhibits a rate of enjambment of 50%. This, however, is a poem and not a performance text, such as a masque or play, in which the pressure to produce fluid, supple, and extended speech units might be expected to produce higher levels of enjambment. In fact, the unusually high rate of enjambment in the masque might be thought to suggest the involvement of a poet with theatrical experience, since in Foster's study of the elegiac verse of the period 1608–13 the highest rates of enjambment appeared in texts by poets working in the theatre.[36]

In addition to this adeptness at and high level of enjambment, the masque also exhibits the kind of idiosyncratic, obscure, or careless phrasing for which Chapman's verse is notorious.[37] In fact, the most awkward instance of phrasing in the masque—a strange, tortured phrase with a horrible rhyme ("till to bee vertuous | Bee held a greater guilt then to bee us," lines 72–73)—echoes a similarly awkward turn from Chapman's "Hymnus in Cynthiam" (1598): "Deare Goddesse, prompt, benigne, and bounteous, | That heares all prayers, from the least of us" (lines 202–03). That this may be an unintentional echo rather than a deliberate borrowing can hardly be in doubt: what poet would ever attempt to imitate such a rhyme? Other parallels of rhyme may be noticed, though none are particularly striking.[38]

Orthographic evidence provides a basis for associating Chapman with the masque. Although there are too few Chapman holographs to be of much help in examining the orthography of the masque text (which is not, in any case, in Chapman's hand), certain distinctive features are shared by the text and the printed works of Chapman.[39] Such evidence, however, must of course be taken cautiously, given the habitual interference of both scribes and compositors with the orthography of their copy. First, the highly unusual forms "maske," "maskers," and "Antemaskers," which appear in the masque text, are paralleled in the first printed quarto of Chapman's *Memorable Masque* (1613), which contains the forms "Maske" and "Antemaske."[40] This is a significant connection: these spellings were unusual (unusual enough to be corrected in the second quarto to the more conventional "Masque" and "Anti-masque"); the form "antemaske" in particular appears to have been almost unique to Chapman.[41] Although "maske" was not itself a particularly uncommon spelling, few writers other than Chapman favored the prefix "ante." It appears in Daniel's *Tethys' Festival*, in Middleton's *Inner Temple Masque, or Masque of Heroes*, in Robert White's *Cupid's Banishment*, in Townshend's *Florimène*, and in the anonymous *Masque of the Twelve Months*—a work plausibly attributed to Chapman by Martin Butler.[42] Only in *The*

Memorable Masque, The Essex House Masque, and *Cupid's Banishment* does the combination of "Ante" and "maske" appear.

Similar parallels may be found between the linguistic features of the masque text and the stylistically elevated and "conservative linguistic pattern" identified by Cyrus Hoy as characteristic of Chapman's tragedies. Hoy observes that Chapman, in his tragedies, regularly prefers the older forms "hath" and "doth" over "has" and "does," and he abbreviates sparingly, making regular use only of "t'" for "to."[43] These tendencies are exhibited in the masque: "hath" appears three times and "has" never; "doth" makes seven appearances and "does," none. As one would expect in so dignified a masque, few abbreviations are employed: "t'" for "to" is used just twice. And yet scribes and compositors, imposing their own preferences on their copy, may well have polluted this evidence to some undeterminable degree.[44] It cannot form a firm basis for attribution.

One of the more promising uses of linguistic evidence in attribution is to consider an early-modern writer's use of auxiliary or periphrastic "do." Jonathan Hope has demonstrated that a writer's tendency to regulate the use of auxiliary or periphrastic "do" by omitting it tends to be fairly consistent and individually distinctive over a broad temporal range. Hope has used this method with success in analyzing various plays from the Shakespeare apocrypha. Unfortunately, however, there are problems in subjecting the masque to this kind of statistical analysis. First, the text yields a sample that is on the low end of adequate, providing only 57 tokens to Hope's minimum recommended sample of 50.[45] As such, the results are closer to those we might gain from an individual scene than they are to those of a complete play. The problem here is that, as Hope shows (22–24), the rate of regulation can vary quite widely (by as much as 10%) from scene to scene. Herein lies our second problem: the lack of an adequate base for comparison. A high level of formality and the use of verse are likely to yield a higher rate of auxiliary usage.[46] This suggests both that Chapman's plays are unlikely to serve as valuable comparators with a court masque, and that the evidence provided by Chapman's own *Memorable Masque,* which, unlike *The Essex House Masque,* contains a large amount of prose, needs to be handled with some caution. The final section of *The Memorable Masque* (lines 190–418) is written primarily in verse and provides us with 65 tokens: these yield a regulation rate of 88%; the rate of regulation in *The Essex House Masque* is 82%.[47] The two rates are close enough not to discount the possibility of common authorship, but not so close as to confirm it.

The strongest evidence for Chapman's authorship lies in the parallels between his idiosyncratic word use and the lexical peculiarities of the masque. The most striking instance of Chapmanesque phrasing in the masque appears in the song accompanying the revelation of the masquers. "Then veiw the spring of man begun | By your one sun" (lines 208–09), urges the song. "Spring of man" is an attractive phrase; but what does it mean? It seems to refer in part to the youth of the masquers: these are men in their spring. But its formulation does not highlight such a reading; "men of spring" would do better. The meaning of the phrase hinges on the particular kind of "spring" we are invited to view. What the audience has witnessed in the revelation of the main masque is not just a group of young men, but the creation of the human race. In this context, it is clear that the term "spring" is used in a now rare sense: "A springing up, growing, or bursting forth of plants, vegetation, etc.; a growth or crop; also, a race or stock of persons" (*OED, sb.*[1] III.11). The first recorded application of the term "spring" to denote a race is in Chapman's version of the pseudo-Homeric "Hymn of Apollo" (1624?): "Typhon, who on all the humane Spring | Confer'd confusion" (lines 554–55).[48] And it looks very much as if the masque employs the term in this manner. In the masque, the phrase "spring of man" denotes not only the bursting forth of life from the rock, it also denotes that we are witnessing the origins of the human race. In both the hymn and the masque, then, the term "spring" appears to refer both to the human race and to imply its youth—an innovative usage apparently peculiar to Chapman.

Not only did Chapman use the term "spring" in the unusual sense in which it also appears in the masque, he also used the distinctive phrase "spring of man" on two additional occasions. In his *Epicede or Funerall Song: On the most disastrous Death, of the High-borne Prince of Men, Henry Prince of Wales, &c.* (1612), Chapman referred to his short-lived patron, Prince Henry, as "this spring of Man" (line 461). A decade later (but only 18 months or so after *The Essex House Masque*), Chapman returned to the phrase in his *Pro Vere, Autumni Lachrymae* (1622), a lament for the beleaguered general, Horace Vere, then "Beseiged and distrest" in Manheim, where he was fighting for the protestant cause. Vere's name (suggesting the Latin word for spring) presented the poet with an irresistible point of departure: it is autumn, yet Vere is "this full Spring of Man" (line 2). Although in neither of these two instances does the term "spring" function in quite the manner of the hymn or the masque, it was a favorite phrase of Chapman, and this corroborates its value as a mark of his authorship.[49] That value is further corroborated by its rarity: I have found only two other uses of the phrase in texts from this period, both of which employ the term "spring" in the thoroughly conventional sense of beginning or origin.[50] The phrase appears in Robert Greene's *Perimedes* (1588) ("It fits that youth the spring of man should be"), and in Middleton's *More Dissemblers Besides Women* (c. 1615?) ("continence, I . . . is a rare grace in the spring of man").[51]

Another instance of peculiarly Chapmanesque word use appears in the opening song. Announcing the first antimasque—a dance of beasts—Tellus insists that "the mynes of mocion must pertake I Which neyther growth nor earthquake make" (lines 27–28). The fact that she means by "mynes" something other than repositories of mineral wealth is apparent both from her own denial that this motion will produce growth (the means by which minerals were thought to be generated), as well as from the lack of any reference to precious metals in the masque. Tellus uses the term "mynes" in the very unusual sense of "subterranean cavities," a usage so rare that *OED* cites only two instances of it: one in Shakespeare's *Othello*, and the other in Chapman's version of *Homer's Iliads* (*OED*, *sb.* 1.d). That Tellus is using the term in this way is confirmed by the opening song, which alludes to "the hollow Earth," and by the stage direction, which indicates that as the first antimasque departs a cave is revealed, "*from whence issue .9. giants the supposed sonnes and champions of the earth*" (lines 37–38).

Other striking phrases from the masque are paralleled in the poetry of Chapman. "The sparkles of the morninge" that shine in Prometheus's speech (line 160) chime with "the sparckles of the night" from Chapman's "Hymnus in Cynthiam" (line 395). And the reference in the last song to the dancing couples, "Like aire | Fillinge each place" (lines 232–33), resonates with Chapman's injunction to Somerset in the dedicatory epistle to *Andromeda Liberata* (1614): "Like Aire, fill every corner of your place" (line 107). Although these parallels are distinctive, they are not demonstrably exclusive to the writings of Chapman on the one hand and *The Essex House Masque* on the other; they are, as such, of limited value as evidence for attribution.[52]

A firm attribution would, of course, require more than merely internal evidence. The most I can offer by way of external evidence is some circumstantial connections between Chapman and Doncaster at about the time of the masque. Little is known about Chapman's life at that time. We do, however, know that he surfaced in London in the middle of 1620, after several years in hiding due to an ongoing lawsuit against him. Chapman's countersuit was first heard in London in June 1620, and the case was resolved in February 1622.[53] The evidence suggests therefore that he was based in the capital during the period leading up to the masque and that he was, as usual, in financial distress.[54] Biographical evidence thus gives us every reason to imagine that his financial circumstances would have rendered a commission to write a masque in the winter of 1620–21 an attractive one. But whence might such a commission have derived?

A commission might have reached Chapman by several routes. Although we know of no direct connection between Chapman and Doncaster, there are several points of mutual contact. One of these might have been the Royal Academy project of Edmund Bolton, a project with which Doncaster's masque might have been aligned. Bolton praised Chapman's *Iliads* for its "Brave language" in his *Hypercritica* (c.1618?), and, in a later proposal for his academy (1626), he named Chapman as a potential member.[55] There are still closer connections. During the years immediately preceding the masque, Chapman's long standing patron, Robert Carr, first earl of Somerset, was committed to the Tower of London. Chapman continued to dedicate works to him during his imprisonment and after his release in 1622.[56] Chapman knew Carr, and Carr knew Doncaster: indeed, Carr apparently owed his meteoric rise at court to Doncaster, and he employed him as his intermediary in the period leading up to his trial in 1616.[57] Also in the Tower at this time, and much in the company of Carr and his wife, was Henry Percy, ninth earl of Northumberland: another figure known to both Chapman and Doncaster.[58] Doncaster had married Northumberland's daughter in 1617, and the two men subsequently developed an affectionate relationship. Northumberland was known to Chapman as the patron of several of his close associates, including Matthew Roydon, Thomas Harriot, and Robert Hues—the last two of whom offered helpful critiques of Chapman's work on Homer.[59]

Chapman appears to have presented a copy of his *Whole Works of Homer* to Northumberland, who owned several of Chapman's other Homeric translations, including a copy of *The Iliads* which he kept with him in the Tower.[60] Northumberland's client, Harriot, affords another possible link between Chapman and Doncaster: from 1614 until his death in 1621, Harriot lived at Syon House, Northumberland's residence in Isleworth.[61] After his marriage to the earl's daughter, Doncaster took up residence at Essex House, a Percy property, where Harriot also had rooms; he also spent time at Syon House: in September 1620, for example, he entertained Buckingham and his family to a feast there.[62] The Tower, Essex House, and Syon House, Northumberland and Somerset: any one of these points of mutual contact may have served to bring Chapman to Doncaster's attention at the time of the masque.[63]

There is, in sum, sufficient internal evidence to posit the possibility of Chapman's authorship of the masque, but not enough to provide a firm attribution. Several distinct strands of evidence point in his direction: favored themes, stylistic strengths, stylistic weaknesses, idiosyncratic orthography, linguistic preferences, and, above all, highly unusual word use. Biographical evidence provides circumstantial corroboration: there were several points of potential contact between poet and patron. We might add that the pro-Protestant slant of the masque squares with the sympathies Chapman expressed in such works as *Pro Vere*, and that the attack on Jonson meshes with what little we know about the breakdown of relations between the two men—perhaps revealing the origins of their acrimony.[64] The attribution of the masque to Chapman would also square with my tentative identification of Jones as its designer and inventor. Jones and Chapman had collaborated before. For *The Memorable Masque* of 1613, Chapman had, as the title page of its printed text announces, *"Supplied, Aplied, Digested, and written"* a text to body forth Jones's invention.[65] Not for this poet any struggle for precedence with the architect. The two men continued to be close. Jones probably designed the handsome title page for Chapman's *Whole Works of Homer*; in 1616 Chapman dedicated his translation of Musaeus to Jones in the warmest terms; and Jones would later design Chapman's funeral monument.[66] The two were, moreover, in later years firmly allied in their hostility to Jonson: in 1634 or thereabouts Chapman composed a scabrous poetic attack on Jonson in response to his badmouthing of Jones.[67]

Such speculations might help to confirm a case that was in need of corroboration only; they do not, however, provide firm evidence for such a case. Without additional evidence (preferably external or documentary—a payment, perhaps, or a reference in a letter), the case for Chapman and Jones as inventors of the masque can only be regarded as, at best, a plausible hypothesis.

NOTES

Notes to Textual Introduction

1. John Nichols, *The Progresses, Processions, and Magnificent Entries of James the First*, 4 vols. (London, 1828), 4:647; Paul Reyher, *Les Masques Anglais: Étude sur les Ballets et la vie de Cour en Angleterre (1512–1640)* (Paris: Hachette, 1909), 95; Mary Susan Steele, *Plays & Masques at Court during the Reigns of Elizabeth, James and Charles* (New Haven and London: Yale University Press, 1926), 210; Gerald Eades Bentley, *The Jacobean and Caroline Stage*, 7 vols. (Oxford: Clarendon Press, 1941–68), 7:39; C. E. McGee and John C. Meagher, "Preliminary Checklist of Tudor and Stuart Entertainments: 1614–1625," *Research Opportunities in Renaissance Drama* 30 (1988): 17–128 (89, 92).

2. No text is mentioned in W. W. Greg's *A List of Masques, Pageants, &c.* (London: Bibliographical Society, 1902), or in Gertrude Marion Sibley's *The Lost Plays and Masques 1500–1642* (1931; reprint, New York: Russell & Russell, 1971). For the first discussion of the text, see Timothy Raylor "The 'Lost' *Essex House Masque* (1621): A Manuscript Text Discovered," *English Manuscript Studies 1100–1700* 7 (1998): 86–130.

3. Enid Welsford, *The Court Masque: A Study in the Relationship between Poetry & the Revels* (Cambridge: Cambridge University Press, 1927), 198, 203.

4. This paragraph draws upon the full discussion of Doncaster's masques offered below in chapter 1: "Viscount Doncaster and his Magnificent Entertainments."

5. James Knowles, "The 'Running Masque' Recovered?: A Masque for the Marquess of Buckingham," *English Manuscript Studies 1100–1700* 8 (1999).

6. McGee and Meagher, "Preliminary Check-list," 54.

7. See below, chapter 1: "Viscount Doncaster and his Magnificent Entertainments." Both William Browne's *Masque of the Inner Temple* (1615) and James Shirley's *The Triumph of Peace* (1634) featured dances of nine antimasquers; in *A Masque of the Nine Passions* (1597–98[?]) nine masquers had burst out of a heart (Steele, *Plays & Masques at Court,* 114–15); and Thomas Middleton's *Inner Temple Masque, or Masque of Heroes* (1619) included a masque of nine heroes who are generally identified as the Nine Worthies—figures who also made an appearance in his and Rowley's *Courtly Masque: The Device, called The World tost at Tennis* (1619–20); *The Inner Temple Masque, or Masque of Heroes,* ed. R. C. Bald, in T. J. B. Spencer and Stanley Wells, gen. eds., *A Book of Masques: In Honour of Allardyce Nicoll* (Cambridge: Cambridge University Press, 1967), 255–56.

8. *Finetti Philoxenis* (London, 1656), 72.

9. I have explored the question of the identity of the son in "Who Danced in *The Essex House Masque* (1621)?" *Notes & Queries,* new series 44 (1997): 530–33. There is no evidence for regular masquing on the part of any of the Holles boys.

10. Gervase's grandfather was the younger brother of John Holles's father; *The Letters of John Holles, 1587–1637,* ed. P. R. Seddon, 3 vols., Thoroton Society Record Series 31, 35, and 36 (Nottingham, 1975, 1983, and 1986), 1:x. On Gervase Holles, see G[ordon] G[oodwin], "Holles, Gervase (1606–1675)," *DNB;* R. W. Goulding, "Gervase Holles, a great lover of antiquities," *Transactions of the Thoroton Society* 26 (1922): 36–70. Holles's family history was edited and published as *Memorials of the Holles Family 1493–1656,* ed. A. C. Wood, Camden Society, 3d series, 55 (London, 1937).

11. A full description of the manuscript, distinguishing the several hands which appear in it, and attending to its binding, paper, foliation, contents, and provenance is offered in my "The 'Lost' *Essex House Masque,*" 95–110.

12. See my "The 'Lost' *Essex House Masque,*" 102, 107.

13. Cf. the copy of *The Masque of Proteus* discussed by Stephen Orgel, *The Jonsonian Masque* (Cambridge, Mass.: Harvard University Press, 1965), 17.

14. From the first earl's correspondence we know that he was resident there in December 1622, and had been so for some time; *Letters of John Holles,* 2:259, 270. He was still there in the winter of 1626; *Memorials,* 228.

15. Souvenir or presentation copies were sometimes printed, but were often copied and distributed in manuscript form; see John C. Meagher, *Method and Meaning in Jonson's Masques* (Notre Dame, Ind. and London: University of Notre Dame Press, 1966), 202, note

99; Peter Walls, "Insubstantial Pageants Preserved: the Literary and Musical Sources for the Jonsonian Masque," in Ian Donaldson, ed., *Jonson and Shakespeare* (Atlantic Highlands, N. J.: Humanities Press, 1983), 202–18 (204–07); James Knowles, "Marston, Skipwith and *The Entertainment at Ashby*," *English Manuscript Studies 1100–1700*, 3 (1992): 137–92 (145–46).

16. It is perhaps worth noting, however, that Holles and his associates ranged widely in their historical researches, consulting manuscripts from many sources: these included the Bodleian Library, the Pipe Rolls Office, the antiquaries Roger Dodsworth and William Dugdale, and the private libraries of Sir Christopher Hatton, and Sir Gervase Clifton; BL, Lansdowne MSS 207 B, fols. 203r, 309r; 207 E, fols. 69r, 255r; *Memorials*, 22, 43, 61, 133, 138, 170.

17. See A. C. Partridge, *Orthography in Shakespeare and Elizabethan Drama: A Study of Colloquial Contractions, Elision, Prosody and Punctuation* (Lincoln, Nebr.: University of Nebraska Press, 1964), 75–78.

18. It seems possible that B's use of capital "A" derives from a misreading of a "spurred" secretary "a" such as was used by George Chapman; see Anthony G. Petti, *English Literary Hands from Chaucer to Dryden* (Cambridge, Mass.: Harvard University Press, 1977), 92–93; number 41.

19. Anthony Graham-White, *Punctuation and its Dramatic Value in Shakespearean Drama* (Newark, Del.: University of Delaware Press; London: Associated University Presses, 1995), 29–30.

20. The use of punctuation marks in the text is broadly in line with the patterns described in Partridge, *Orthography in Shakespeare*, 124–40; Mindele Treip, *Milton's Punctuation and Changing English Usage 1582–1676* (London: Methuen, 1970), chapters 2–3 (14–53); and Graham-White, *Punctuation and its Dramatic Value*, 29–30.

21. M. B. Parkes makes the important point that this is generally true in *Pause and Effect: An Introduction to the History of Punctuation in the West* (Berkeley and Los Angeles: University of California Press, 1993), 2.

22. Partridge, *Orthography in Shakespeare*, 192.

23. See also line 93, where the problem appears earlier, and line 201, where a different configuration presents a similar problem.

24. Such marks were often used interchangeably, and are frequently hard to distinguish from one another; Anne Lancashire, ed., *The Second Maiden's Tragedy* (Manchester: Manchester University Press; Baltimore: Johns Hopkins University Press, 1978), 61; Graham-White, *Punctuation and its Dramatic Value*, 31–35.

Notes to Chapter One

1. Charles ran against the earl of Dorset; the marquess of Buckingham against the earl of Montgomery; and the marquess of Hamilton against the earl of Warwick; *The Autobiography and Correspondence of Sir Simonds D'Ewes,* ed. James Orchard Halliwell, 2 vols. (London, 1845), 1:166.

2. *CSPD 1619–1623,* 202.

3. A list of personnel survives in PRO, SP 78/68, fols. 312–13.

4. Finett, *Finetti Philoxenis* (London, 1656), 67–68.

5. *CSPD 1619–1623,* 199, 201.

6. *Autobiography and Correspondence of Sir Simonds D'Ewes,* 1:167; Chamberlain, 2:331; *CSPVen. 1619–1621,* 533–34.

7. PRO, E 351/544, fols. 131v, 135r (King's Chamber Accounts). Jones was paid for his work on 21 June 1621; Malone Society, "Dramatic Records in the Declared Accounts of the Treasurer of the Chamber 1588–1642," *Collections* 6 (1961 [1962]): 134–35.

8. PRO, E 351/544, fol. 131r (King's Chamber Accounts); Malone Society, *Collections* 6 (1961 [1962]): 118–19.

9. Finett, *Finetti Philoxenis,* 68–69.

10. "Upon the French Embassadours enterteinement in England at W. Hall Dec. 30 1620," Houghton Library, Harvard University, MS Eng 686, fol. 20v; Jean Beaulieu to William Trumbull, 4/14 January 1620/21; BL, Trumbull Correspondence, MS VII, number 1.

11. Finett, *Finetti Philoxenis,* 69; *CSPD 1619–1623,* 204.

12. Finett, *Finetti Philoxenis,* 69–70; Chamberlain, 2:333.

13. Martin Butler, "Ben Jonson's *Pan's Anniversary* and the Politics of Early Stuart Pastoral," *English Literary Renaissance* 22 (1992): 369–404.

14. "Upon the French Embassadours enterteinement in England at W. Hall Dec. 30 1620," Houghton Library, Harvard University, MS Eng 686, fol. 20v.

15. Arthur Wilson, *The History of Great Britain: being the life and reign of King James the First* (London, 1653), 92.

16. G. P. V. Akrigg offers a succinct discussion of the phenomenon of the favorite in *Jacobean Pageant or The Court of King James I* (Cambridge, Mass.: Harvard University Press, 1963), 178–79; *The Letters of Elizabeth Queen of Bohemia,* comp. L. M. Baker, intro. C. V. Wedgwood (London: Bodley Head, 1953), 81; Schreiber, 8.

17. Wilson, *History,* 154; S[amuel] R[awson] G[ardiner], "Hay, James, first Earl of Carlisle, first Viscount Doncaster, and first Baron Hay (d. 1636)," *DNB*; Schreiber.

18. Schreiber; Samuel Rawson Gardiner, *A History of England*

under the Duke of Buckingham and Charles I: 1625–1628, 2 vols. (London, 1875), 2:177, 259, note 1.

19. Simon Adams, "Foreign Policy and the Parliaments of 1621 and 1624," in Kevin Sharpe, ed., *Faction and Parliament: Essays on Early Stuart History* (Oxford: Oxford University Press, 1978; reprint, London and New York: Methuen, 1985), 139–71 (142–46, 156–58).

20. Schreiber, 30, 35, 40–41; Paul R. Sellin, *"So Doth, So Is Religion": John Donne and Diplomatic Contexts in the Reformed Netherlands, 1619–1620* (Columbia, Mo.: University of Missouri Press, 1988). On his continued interest in the cause, see his correspondence in British Library, Egerton MSS 2592–97, *passim*.

21. François de Bassompierre, *Negociation du Mareschal de Bassompierre envoyé Ambassadeur Extraordinaire, en Angleterre . . . 1626* (Cologne, 1668), 221.

22. Schreiber, 6. After the perceived mistreatment of his 1622 embassy to France, he became increasingly willing to take a tough stance in negotiations with them, as his conduct of the marriage negotiations makes clear; Schreiber, 48; Gardiner, *History of England under the Duke of Buckingham*, 1:89–90, 98, 108, 176–77.

23. *The Letters of Peter Paul Rubens*, trans. and ed. Ruth Saunders Magurn (Cambridge, Mass.: Harvard University Press, 1955), 271–72.

24. Wilson, *History*, 94; Schreiber, 13–15; Chamberlain, 2:13–14.

25. Sir Thomas Edmondes to Sir Ralph Winwood, 27 July 1616; PRO, SP 78/66, fol. 25.

26. Wilson, *History*, 92.

27. Edward [Hyde], earl of Clarendon, *The History of the Rebellion and Civil Wars in England*, ed. W. Dunn Macray, 6 vols. (Oxford, 1888), 1:77.

28. Schedule of Creditors of the first earl of Carlisle, House of Lords Record Office, Main Papers, 18 January 1640/41.

29. Wilson, *History*, 93.

30. Wilson, *History*, 94; Chamberlain, 2:55–56.

31. [Francis Osborne], *Historical Memoires on the Reign of Queen Elizabeth, and King James* (London, 1658), "Traditional Memoyres on the Raigne of King James," 124–25; Gardiner, "Hay," *DNB*; Robert Ashton, ed., *James I by his Contemporaries* (London: Hutchinson, 1969), 232–33; Schreiber, 5, 11, *et passim*.

32. Although the existence of the antesupper has been widely accepted by modern historians, Osborne's account provides the sole witness for the term cited in *OED*. One wonders whether Osborne's account does not derive from a misunderstanding or misrepresentation of the imported fashion for "antipastes."

33. [Osborne], *Historical Memoires*, 126.

34. Alan R. Young, *The English Tournament Imprese* (New York: AMS, 1988), 111; number 367.

35. His efforts to complete by purchase the set of tapestries presented to him on his embassy to the Low Countries in 1619—tapestries designed by François Spierinx, depicting scenes from the *Orlando Furioso*—are discussed by Sellin, *"So Doth, So Is Religion"*, 150–53, 248–51. See also, PRO SP 78/98, fols. 28–29, a letter from Doncaster to Dudley Carleton, 9 November 1620.

36. The gift of the painting and its provenance are noticed in "Abraham van der Doort's Catalogue of the Collections of Charles I," ed. Oliver Millar, *The Walpole Society*, 37 (1958–60 [1960]), 89, 211.

37. Donne's relationship with Doncaster is meticulously traced by R. C. Bald in *John Donne: A Life* (Oxford: Clarendon Press, 1970), 160–62, 272–73, 289, 292–93, 304, 367, 385, 396–97, 410, 431, 448, 471, 474, 488, 493, 523; see also Sellin, *"So Doth, So Is Religion"*.

38. Dedications to Doncaster include Davies's *Bien Venu* (London, 1606), Ayton's *Basia* (London, 1606), Sylvester's *The Second Session of Parliament of Vertues Real* (London, 1615), Weckherlin's *A Panegyricke To the most honourable and renowned Lord, The Lord Hays* (Stuttgart, 1619), Leech's "Epigrammata" (the final section of his *Musæ Priores, sive Poematum Pars Prior* (London, 1620)) and Johnston's *Musæ Querulæ, de Regis in Scotiam Profectione* (London, 1633). A manuscript copy of John Ford's *Linea Vitae. A Line of Life* is dedicated to Hay (BL, Lansdowne MS 350, fols. 139–78]: see *The Nondramatic Works of John Ford*, ed. L. E. Stock, Gilles P. Monsarrat, Judith M. Kennedy, and Dennis Danielson (Binghamton, N. Y.: Medieval & Renaissance Texts & Studies, 1991), 302. Poems to Hay and his family appear in Nicholas Oldisworth's "Recollection of Certain Scattered Poems" (1644), Bodleian Library, Oxford, MS Don. C. 24, fol. 11v; in Craig's *Poetical Recreations* (Edinburgh, 1609), 11, 17–18 and in his *Poetical Recreations* (Aberdeen, 1623), 29; in Johnston's *Epigrammata* (Aberdeen, 1632), 10; and in Leech's "Epigrammata," at least one of which dates from 1621 (8, 29, 53, 76, 81, 82). On connections between members of this Scottish circle, see *The Poetical Works of Alexander Craig of Rose-Craig 1604–1631*, intro. David Laing (Glasgow, 1872), 10, 16; *The English and Latin Poems of Sir Robert Ayton*, ed. Charles B. Gullans, Scottish Text Society, 4th series, 1 (Edinburgh, 1963), 18–19, 45–48, 170, 171, 223–30; Leech, "Epigrammata," 42, 52, 61.

39. *Autobiography of Thomas Raymond*, ed. G. Davies, Camden Society, 3d series, 28 (London, 1917), 25.

40. HMC 9, *Salisbury (Cecil) Manuscripts*, 24: *Addenda 1605–1668*, ed. G. Dyfnallt Owen (London: HMSO, 1976), 270.

41. *Ben Jonson*, 10:433, 482; *The Works of Thomas Campion*, ed. Walter R. Davis (New York: Doubleday, 1967; reprint, London: Faber, 1969), 284; Orgel and Strong, 1:105, 241.

42. *CSPVen. 1619–1621*, 390, note; Martin Butler, "Jonson's *News from the New World*, the 'Running Masque', and the Season of 1619–20," *Medieval & Renaissance Drama in England* 6 (1993): 153–78 (161); *Autobiography of Thomas Raymond*, 25. Hay's son was apparently scheduled to have appeared in *Pleasure Reconciled to Virtue* (1618) but did not do so—perhaps as a result of the royal displeasure over *The Masque of Amazons*; *Ben Jonson*, 10:575. He later appeared in *Love's Triumph Through Callipolis* (1631), *Albion's Triumph* (1632), *The Temple of Love* (1635), *Britannia Triumphans* (1638), *Luminalia* (1638), and *Salmacida Spolia* (1640); Orgel and Strong, 1:405, 2:453, 599, 661, 705, 729.

43. On voids and banquets, see C. Anne Wilson, "The Evolution of the Banquet Course: Some Medicinal, Culinary and Social Aspects," in C. Anne Wilson, ed., *"Banquetting Stuffe": The Fare and Social Background of the Tudor and Stuart Banquet* (Edinburgh: Edinburgh University Press, 1991), 9–35. The association of masques and feasts was conventional; Allardyce Nicoll, *Stuart Masques and the Renaissance Stage* (London: Harrap, 1938), 29–32; Patricia Fumerton, *Cultural Aesthetics: Renaissance Life and the Practice of Cultural Ornament* (Chicago and London: University of Chicago Press, 1991), chapter 4 (111–67).

44. The location of *Lovers Made Men* was indicated by contemporary accounts, and implied by Jonson's printed text, which noted that it was performed at Hay's house (Hay was resident in the Wardrobe until his resignation from the mastership in 1618); Chamberlain, 2:55; Schreiber, 21, 149; T. J. B. Spencer and Stanley Wells, gen. eds., *A Book of Masques: In Honour of Allardyce Nicoll* (Cambridge: Cambridge University Press, 1967), 209–10.

45. *Letters from George Carew to Sir Thomas Roe*, ed. John Maclean, Camden Society 76 (London, 1860), 92; HMC 75, *Report on the Manuscripts of the Most Honourable the Marquess of Downshire formerly at Easthampstead Park, Berkshire, 6: Papers of William Trumbull the Elder, September 1616—December 1618*, ed. G. Dyfnallt Owen and Sonia P. Anderson (London: HMSO, 1995), 119; McGee and Meagher, "Preliminary Checklist of Tudor and Stuart Entertainments: 1614–1625," *Research Opportunities in Renaissance Drama* 30 (1988): 17–128 (47–48). Anthony Weldon's account of the entertainment of baron le Tour in *The Court and Character of King James* (London, 1650), 19–20, appears, as Stanley Wells suggests, to

muddle this and the entertainment of 1621; Spencer and Wells, gen. eds., *A Book of Masques*, 210, note 1.

46. Chamberlain, 2:57–58; Spencer and Wells, gen. eds., *A Book of Masques*, 209–10.

47. Paul Reyher, *Les Masques Anglais: Étude sur les Ballets et la vie de Cour en Angleterre (1512–1640)* (Paris: Hachette, 1909), 524; Mary Susan Steele, *Plays & Masques at Court during the Reigns of Elizabeth, James and Charles* (New Haven: Yale University Press, 1926), 200; Gerald Eades Bentley, *The Jacobean and Caroline Stage*, 7 vols. (Oxford: Clarendon Press, 1941–68), 5:1288–90; 7:25; McGee and Meagher, "Preliminary Checklist," 54; Chamberlain, 2:126.

48. The masquers included Lady Hay and her sister, Dorothy; Barbara Sidney; the wives of Sir Robert and Sir Henry Rich, and Isabella Rich; Chamberlain, 2:126. On the politics of the group, see Adams, "Foreign Policy and the Parliaments of 1621 and 1624," 145–46. Butler, however, suggests that the masque may have been cancelled because of fears that it might upstage the king's Twelfth Night masque; "Jonson's *News from the New World*," 161.

49. *CSPD 1619–1623*, 112; Butler, "Jonson's *News from the New World*," 159, 161, 165, 172, 173, 174; John Orrell, "The London Court Stage in the Savoy Correspondence, 1613–1675," *Theatre Research International* 4 (1979): 79–94 (87); McGee and Meagher, "Preliminary Checklist," 74–76.

50. Orgel and Strong, 1:115; David Lindley, "Who paid for Campion's *Lord Hay's Masque*?," *Notes & Queries*, new series, 26 (1979): 144–45.

51. *Works of Campion*, 232; Graham Parry, *The Golden Age Restor'd: The Culture of the Stuart Court, 1603–42* (Manchester: Manchester University Press, 1981), 97; David Lindley, *Thomas Campion* (Leiden: Brill, 1989), 191. Hay was in particular charge of providing Elizabeth's apparel for the wedding; Arthur Wilson, *The Narrative History of King James, for the first fourteen Years* (London, 1651), 14.

52. Jonson's use of this theme is explored by John C. Meagher, *Method and Meaning in Jonson's Masques* (Notre Dame, Ind. and London: University of Notre Dame Press, 1966), chapter 6 (125–43).

53. *Works of Campion*, 221–22.

54. *Ben Jonson*, 2:302; 10:568; Stanley Wells, ed., Jonson, *Lovers Made Men*, in Spencer and Wells, gen. eds., *A Book of Masques*, 210.

55. Stephen Orgel, *The Jonsonian Masque* (Cambridge, Mass.: Harvard University Press, 1965), 128.

56. James Knowles, "Change Partners and Dance: A Newly Discovered Jacobean Masque," *Times Literary Supplement*, 9 August 1991, 19.

57. Reporting on the day of *Lovers Made Men*, the Florentine agent in London noted that 11 noblemen were expected to dance that night; McGee and Meagher, "Preliminary Checklist," 47.

58. *Ben Jonson*, 2:301–02.

59. *Works of Campion*, 213.

60. The musicians, including nine violinists, three lutenists, six cornets and six singers, were disposed in a triangle in front of the stage; a raised stage (three feet higher than the main stage) was placed 18 feet from the screen; *Works of Campion*, 211. On the tripartite structure of the masque, see Lindley, *Thomas Campion*, 179.

61. Chamberlain, 2:125; McGee and Meagher, "Preliminary Checklist," 54.

62. Chamberlain, 2:13–14.

63. Canova-Green, 42–43.

64. Enid Welsford, *The Court Masque: A Study in the Relationship between Poetry & the Revels* (Cambridge: Cambridge University Press, 1927); John Peacock, "The French Element in Inigo Jones's Masque Designs," in David Lindley, ed., *The Court Masque* (Manchester: Manchester University Press, 1984), 149–68; see also, John Peacock, *The Stage Designs of Inigo Jones: The European Context* (Cambridge: Cambridge University Press, 1995), 240–66.

65. Jonson's ownership of a copy of the *Balet Comique* and its influence on his masques has been explored by Meagher in *Method and Meaning in Jonson's Masques*, 22–30, *et passim*; its influence on masques by Campion and Townshend has been noted by Margaret M. McGowan in *L'Art du Ballet de Cour en France 1581–1643* (Paris: CNRS, 1963), 241–45 (244). Beaujoyeulx was in fact Italian, and his work is in the Italian style of court entertainment.

66. Canova-Green noted his innovativeness in this respect, primarily on the basis of the use of recitative in *Lovers Made Men*, 214.

67. "A la lovange de Monsieur de Hay ode," PRO SP 14/198/20.

68. Canova-Green, 196–97; McGee and Meagher, "Preliminary Checklist," 46. In the address to the king attached to the printed text of his *Ode a la lovange du serenissime Roy de la Grande Bretaigne* (London, 1617), de Mailliet notes that he is well known to both Hay and Lord Aubigny (sig. A1v); the address is not attached to the manuscript copy (presumably the presentation copy in the poet's own hand) in BL, Royal MS 16E.XVIII.

69. See Welsford, *The Court Masque*, 185; Canova-Green, 200, 222. James Knowles and Marie-Claude Canova-Green are currently editing the *ballet*.

70. Letter to author, 26 June 1996.

71. Malone Society, "Dramatic Records in the Declared Accounts of the Office of Works 1560–1640," *Collections* 10 (1975 [1977]): 27;

Malone Society, "Dramatic Records in the Declared Accounts of the Treasurer of the Chamber 1588–1642," *Collections* 6 (1961 [1962]): 62–64.

72. Chamberlain, 2:56.

73. Malherbe, *Œuvres*, ed. Antoine Adam (Paris: Gallimard, 1971), 203; Canova-Green, 203; Jean Jacquot, "Le reine Henriette-Marie et l'influence française dans les spectacles à la cour de Charles Ier," *9e Cahiers de l'association international des études françaises* (1957), 128–60 (134).

74. Schreiber, 101; *CSPVen. 1626–1628*, 107; Canova-Green, 180. I suspect that Gaultier might have been the " French man" employed in 1619 to instruct Doncaster's son in French. In a letter of 10 June 1619, William Woodford, the family chaplain, wrote to inform Doncaster of his sudden disappearance (BL, Egerton MS 2592, fol. 134r)— a disappearance which coincides with French attempts to have Gaultier deported to face trial for his murder of a French nobleman (the French eventually dropped the case, and Gaultier went on to enjoy a career as a court musician). Correspondence about the case, which ran through the summer and autumn of 1619, appears in the letterbook of the English Ambassador at Paris, Edward Herbert: BL, Additional MS 7082, fols. 34r, 40r, 41v, 43r, 64r.

75. Welsford, *The Court Masque*, 205, note 2.

76. Welsford, *The Court Masque*, 181–82; Canova-Green, 240–41; *Euvres en Rime de Ian Antoine de Baif*, ed. Ch. Marty-Laveaux, 5 vols. (Paris, 1881–90), 2:331–42.

77. See Jean Rousset, *La Littérature de l'Age Baroque en France: Circé et le Paon* (Paris: Corti, 1954), chapter 1 (13–31, 261–62). I am grateful to Professor François Laroque for drawing my attention to this work. The English ballet featuring Orpheus to which Rousset alludes (2, 262) is presumably *The Lords' Masque*.

78. Ben Jonson, *The Complete Masques*, ed. Stephen Orgel (New Haven and London: Yale University Press, 1969), 257–58; *Ben Jonson*, 10:566–68; Andrew J. Sabol, ed., *A Score for Lovers Made Men: A Masque by Ben Jonson* (Providence, R. I.: Brown University Press, 1963), xv–xvii; Meagher, *Method and Meaning in Jonson's Masques*, 78, 196–97, note 62; Peter Walls, "The Origins of English Recitative," *Proceedings of the Royal Musical Association* 110 (1983–84): 25–40; Canova-Green, 214.

79. Paul Lacroix, ed., *Ballets et Mascarades de Cour de Henri III a Louis XIV*, 6 vols. (Geneva and Turin, 1868–70), 2:3–4, 101–19.

80. On the French *ballet*, see McGowan, *L'Art du Ballet de Cour*, 267. There had, however, been an English *Maske of Amazons* in 1578–79; Steele, *Plays & Masques at Court*, 73.

81. Although Essex House was owned by the Earl of Essex,

Doncaster was regularly resident there after his departure from the Wardrobe in 1618; Charles Lethbridge Kingsford, "Essex House, formerly Leicester House and Exeter Inn," *Archaeologia* 73 (1923): 1–54 (13); Schreiber, 140, 149.

82. The most comprehensive narrative of European events of this period, from an English perspective, remains Samuel R. Gardiner, *History of England from the Accession of James I. to the Outbreak of the Civil War 1603–42*, 10 vols. (London, 1883–84), 3:328–92. I have supplemented Gardiner's account with the following works, in addition to those listed in the following notes and bibliography: Akrigg, *Jacobean Pageant*, 334–44; Mary Anne Everett Green, *Elizabeth, Electress Palatine and Queen of Bohemia*, revised by S. C. Lomas (London: Methuen, 1909), 124–76.

83. Gardiner, *History of England*, 3:372, 381.

84. *CSPVen. 1619–1621*, 510, 513–14, 523, 526–27; *CSPD 1619–1623*, 199, 213; Chamberlain, 2:334; Sir George Calvert to Sir Edward Herbert, 14 January 1621, PRO, SP 78/69, fols. 8–10; PRO, PRO 31/3/54, fols. 145–448 (Cadenet's instructions); *Mémoires Inédits du Comte Leveneur de Tillières*, ed. C. Hippeau (Paris, 1863), 28–29; Gardiner, *History of England*, 3:389–90; Charles Howard Carter, *The Secret Diplomacy of the Hapsburgs, 1598–1625* (New York: Columbia University Press, 1964), 182–206; S. L. Adams, "The Road to La Rochelle: English Foreign Policy and the Huguenots, 1610–1629," *Proceedings of the Huguenot Society of London* 22 (1975): 414–29 (421).

85. Gardiner, *History of England*, 3:386–91; Schreiber, 34–37.

86. Jean Beaulieu to William Trumbull, 4/14 January 1620/21; BL, Trumbull Correspondence, MS VII, number 1.

87. *CSPVen. 1619–1621*, 534.

88. Roy E. Schreiber, *The Political Career of Sir Robert Naunton 1589–1635* (London: Royal Historical Society, 1981), 67–83.

89. See, for example, Thomas Gainsford, *Vox Spiritus, or Sir Walter Rawleighs Ghost* (Exeter, England: The Rota, 1983); Simon Adams, "Captain Thomas Gainsford, the 'Vox Spiritus' and the *Vox Populi*," *Bulletin of the Institute of Historical Research* 49 (1976): 141–44.

90. *Stuart Royal Proclamations*, 1: *Royal Proclamations of King James I: 1603–1625*, ed. James F. Larkin and Paul L. Hughes (Oxford: Clarendon Press, 1973), 495–96; number 208.

91. BL, Harleian MS 6103, fols. 12r, 1r, 13v, *et passim*. The scheme is discussed by Ethel M. Portal in "The Academ Roial of King James I," *Proceedings of the British Academy* 7 (1915–16): 189–208 (193); T[homas] C[ooper], "Bolton or Boulton, Edmund (1575?–1633)," *DNB*.

92. *Journals of the House of Lords*, 3:36.

93. McGee and Meagher, "Preliminary Checklist," 72; Chamberlain, 2:233.

94. References are to *The Works of Thomas Middleton*, ed. A. H. Bullen, 8 vols. (London, 1885–86), 7:138–93, and are given parenthetically in the text.

95. The tone of the masque is noted by A. A. Bromham and Zara Bruzzi, The Changeling *and the Years of Crisis, 1619–1624: A Hieroglyph of England* (London and New York: Pinter, 1990), 179–80.

96. It had been intended for performance at "Denmark" (Somerset) House, but was eventually performed professionally by the Prince's Men some time between September 1619 and March 1620; *Works of Thomas Middleton*, 7:139, 141, 147; McGee and Meagher, "Preliminary Checklist," 72–73.

97. Sara Pearl offers a useful general survey of the court masques of the period in "Sounding to present occasions: Jonson's masques of 1620–5," in Lindley, ed., *The Court Masque*, 60–77.

98. Paul R. Sellin, "The Politics of Ben Jonson's *Newes from the New World Discover'd in the Moone*," *Viator* 17 (1986): 321–37; Butler, "Jonson's *News from the New World*," 153–78.

99. My understanding of Jonson's masque has been fundamentally altered by Butler's article, "Ben Jonson's *Pan's Anniversary*."

100. Chamberlain, 2:333.

Notes to Chapter Two

1. Finett, *Finetti Philoxenis*, 72.

2. PRO, E 351/544, fol. 131r (King's Chamber Accounts).

3. Malone Society, "Jacobean and Caroline Revels Accounts, 1603–1642," *Collections* 13 (1986): xiv–xv, 81.

4. *Lovers Made Men* is, as W. Todd Furniss points out, the only one of Jonson's masques in which the transformation does not flow from the king; "Ben Jonson's Masques," in *Three Studies in the Renaissance* (New Haven: Yale University Press, 1958), 89–179 (167–68); quoted by Andrew J. Sabol in *A Score for* Lovers Made Men, xiv, note 9.

5. Schreiber, 58, 92, 101, 105; Samuel Rawson Gardiner, ed., *Letters and Other Documents Illustrating the Relations Between England and Germany at the Commencement of the Thirty Years' War*, Camden Society, 2d series, 98 (London, 1868), 190–92.

6. David Howarth, *Lord Arundel and his Circle* (New Haven and London: Yale University Press, 1985), 156–57, 196–200. Such gift-giving continued throughout the early 1620s: BL, Additional MS 12528

(a transcript of the account book of Sir Sackville Crowe), notes Buckingham's disbursements after staying at Doncaster's residence in 1622 (fol. 6r), and his receipt of a horse from Doncaster in 1624 (fol. 17r).

7. Chamberlain, 2:318–19.

8. Chamberlain, 2:282.

9. Finett, *Finetti Philoxenis*, 72.

10. S[idney] L[ee], "Blount, Lord Mountjoy, and Earl of Newport (1597–1666)," *DNB*; Raylor, "Who Danced in *The Essex House Masque* (1621)?," *Notes & Queries*, new series 44 (1997): 530–33. Hay earlier used some gentlemen who accompanied him on his Paris embassy to dance in *Lovers Made Men*; Chamberlain, 2:56; Canova-Green, 43.

11. *Ben Jonson*, 10:428–29, 433–34.

12. Arthur M. Hind, *Engraving in England in the Sixteenth & Seventeenth Centuries: A Descriptive Catalogue with Introductions, 2: The Reign of James I* (Cambridge: Cambridge University Press, 1955), 2:353–54; plate 188, number 10.

13. He danced in *Love's Triumph Through Callipolis* (1631), *Albion's Triumph* (1632), *The Temple of Love* (1635), *Britannia Triumphans* (1638), and *Salmacida Spolia* (1640); Orgel and Strong, 1:405, 2:453, 599, 661, 729.

14. He appeared in the same masques as Blount (listed in the previous note), with the addition of *Luminalia* (1638); Orgel and Strong, 2:705.

15. Carr had reputedly stood in for Doncaster in a tilt and been wounded in the process; Schreiber, 11. Buckingham's court career was launched by his appearance in a masque at the encouragement of the king; Roger Lockyer, *Buckingham: The Life and Political Career of George Villiers, First Duke of Buckingham 1592–1628* (London and New York: Longman, 1981), 18.

16. Schreiber, 96–98, 101.

17. Lawrence Stone, *The Crisis of the Aristocracy 1558–1641* (Oxford: Clarendon Press, 1965), 561.

18. *Autobiography and Correspondence of Simonds D'Ewes*, 2:167; "Upon the French Embassadours enterteinement in England at W. Hall Dec. 30 1620," Harvard, Houghton MS Eng 686, fol. 20.

19. *CSPVen. 1619–1621*, 533–34.

20. Chamberlain, 2:333–34. Chamberlain's account of the order of events squares with the account of Anthony Weldon in *The Court and Character of King James* (London, 1650), 19–20, who describes an entertainment at Essex House for a French ambassador which involved a lavish supper (featuring muscovy salmon so large that dishes had to be made for them), "a costly Voydee," followed by "a Maske, of choyse Noble-men, and Gentlemen," followed by a

banquet. Weldon, however, thinks that the entertainment was offered to baron le Tour.

21. See above, chapter 1: "Viscount Doncaster and his Magnificent Entertainments."

22. 11/21 January 1620/21; BL, Trumbull Correspondence, MS VII, number 2.

23. The use of ambergris in cookery was primarily a French fashion; C. Anne Wilson, *Food & Drink in Britain from the Stone Age to recent times* (London: Constable, 1973), 356. Doncaster's use of it was notorious; Ashton, ed., *James I by his Contemporaries*, 232–33.

24. Glynne Wickham, *Early English Stages 1300–1660, Vol. 2: 1576–1660* (London: RKP, 1963), 199–200.

25. Kingsford, "Essex House," 21–30. The other possible locations—the Great Chamber over the Hall in the southern extension of the house and the two-storeyed Banqueting House in the southeastern corner of the garden—are less probable, for Chamberlain employs the term "gallerie" to describe the room. The Banqueting House would in any case have been too small to accommodate the kind of table arrangement described by Chamberlain: in a 1590 inventory it is described as containing only a single round table; Kingsford, "Essex House," 23, 51. A gallery had likewise been the setting for the 1607 entertainment of the king and queen at Theobalds; *Ben Jonson*, 7:154.

26. Allardyce Nicoll, *Stuart Masques and the Renaissance Stage* (London: Harrap, 1938), 33–37; Bentley, *Jacobean and Caroline Stage*, 6:263–64; Glynne Wickham, *Early English Stages 1300–1600, Vol. 2.2: 1576–1660* (London: RKP, 1972), 155.

27. A prose argument was issued to accompany *The Masque of Queens* (*Ben Jonson*, 7:318–19); and the distribution of an argument and its reading by the poet were built into the action of the unperformed *Neptune's Triumph; Ben Jonson*, 7:682, 685, 686 (lines 7–8, 125–26, 130–57). Thomas Carew issued a "Designe" to accompany the performance of *Coelum Britannicum; The Poems of Thomas Carew with his Masque* Coelum Britannicum, ed. Rhodes Dunlap (Oxford: Clarendon Press, 1949), 274–75, and Hieronimo presented the more important visitors with an argument of his play in *The Spanish Tragedy;* Thomas Kyd, *The Spanish Tragedy*, ed. Philip Edwards (London: Methuen, 1959), 110 (4.3.5–6). Such texts are discussed by Martin Butler in "Politics and the Masque: *Salmacida Spolia*," in Thomas Healy and Jonathan Sawday, eds. *Literature and the English Civil War* (Cambridge: Cambridge University Press, 1990), 59–74 (74, note 35).

28. Middleton and Rowley, *A Courtly Masque*, lines 252–53.

29. Spencer and Wells, gen. eds., *A Book of Masques*, 267 (lines 323–24).

30. Cf. Claudian, *Gigantomachia*, lines 29–32; *Essex House Masque*, lines 77–81. For further details of parallels and similarities, see the Explanatory Notes to the text of the masque.

31. Aneau's volume was known in England: Jonson imitated a poem from it in *The Forest*; *Ben Jonson*, 11:38.

32. *Ben Jonson*, 10:558 (note on lines 23–24). A burlesque version of the story formed the subject of a college play of the period— *Gigantomachia, or Worke for Jupiter*; Malone Society, "Jacobean Academic Plays," *Collections* 14 (1988): 98–112. In France, an *Intramède du Combat des Dieux et des Géants*, featuring Jupiter, Pallas, and Mercury, had been presented as an interlude to Nicholas Montreiul's *L'Arimene* (1596); Henri Prunières, *Le Ballet de Cour en France avant Benserade et Lully* (1914; reprint, New York: Johnson Reprint, 1970), 147.

33. Christopher White, *Anthony Van Dyck: Thomas Howard The Earl of Arundel* (Malibu, Calif.: Getty Museum, 1995), 58–59.

34. It was identified by John Harris, "The Link between a Roman second-century sculptor, Van Dyck, Inigo Jones and Queen Henrietta Maria," *Burlington Magazine* 115 (1973): 526–30.

35. Harris concluded that the frieze must have belonged to Buckingham at the time of the portrait. Graham Parry and David Howarth objected that since Buckingham was not interested in collecting antique sculpture in 1620 the frieze must have been owned by Arundel, and that the painting must therefore have been commissioned by him for Buckingham, probably as a wedding gift; Parry, *The Golden Age Restor'd*, 139; Howarth, *Lord Arundel and his Circle*, 156–57; Ron Harvie, who presumes that the frieze was in Buckingham's collection at the time, speculates that the painting may have been a present from King James; "A Present from 'Dear Dad'?: Van Dyck's *The Continence of Scipio*," *Apollo* 138 (1993): 224–26; and Christopher White suggests that the incorporation of his own frieze in a painting destined for a rival collector would have been unthinkably tactless on Arundel's part: he concludes that the frieze must therefore have been Buckingham's at the time, moving to Arundel House after his assassination in 1628, and that the painting was commissioned by Buckingham himself; *Anthony Van Dyck: Thomas Howard The Earl of Arundel*, 59–62.

36. Howarth, *Lord Arundel and his Circle*, 197.

37. See, for example, James's dedicatory sonnet to *The Essayes of a Prentise, in the Divine Art of Poesie* (1584), in *The Poems of James VI. of Scotland*, ed. James Craigie, 2 vols., Scottish Text Society, 3d series, 22 and 26 (Edinburgh, 1955 and 1958), 1:3; Francis Bacon's letter to James of 1611; *The Works of Francis Bacon*, ed. James Spedding, Robert Leslie Ellis, and Douglas Denon Heath, 14 vols.

(London, 1857–74), 11:242; and the ceiling of the Whitehall Banqueting House, discussed by D. J. Gordon, "Rubens and the Whitehall Ceiling," in *The Renaissance Imagination*, ed. Stephen Orgel (Berkeley, Los Angeles, and London: University of California Press, 1975), 24–50, and Parry, *The Golden Age Restor'd*, 32–37.

38. Harvie, "A Present from 'Dear Dad'?"; David Kunzle, "Van Dyck's *Continence of Scipio* as a Metaphor of Statecraft at the Early Stuart Court," in John Onians, ed., *Sight and Insight: Essays on Art and Culture in Honour of E. H. Gombrich at 85* (London: Phaidon, 1994), 168–89 (173).

39. Kunzle, "Van Dyck's *Continence of Scipio*," 176; Bacon, *De Sapientia Veterum* (London, 1609), chapter 7.

40. Quoted in Harris, "The Link between a Roman second-century sculptor," 529. See also the parallel note in Jones's copy of Palladio's *I Quattro Libri* (1601); *Inigo Jones on Palladio*, ed. Bruce Allsopp, 2 vols. (Newcastle upon Tyne: Oriel Press, 1970), 2:42. This note postdates the masque: it follows an entry of 23 July 1633.

41. D. E. L. Haynes, *The Arundel Marbles* (Oxford: Ashmolean Museum, 1975), 38–39; plates 14a–b; Haynes, "The Fawley Court Relief," *Apollo* 96 (1972): 6–10.

42. Haynes, *The Arundel Marbles*, 6; Adolf Michaelis, *Ancient Marbles in Great Britain*, trans. C. A. M. Fennell (Cambridge, 1882), 192, 196. The fragment, in fact, appears to come from another source in Asia Minor; Haynes, *The Arundel Marbles*, 20; plate 9.

43. Quoted from Knowles, "The 'Running Masque' Recovered?"

44. This illustration was reproduced in several Italian editions of the *Metamorphoses*; see Olga Raggio, "The Myth of Prometheus: Its Survival and Metamorphoses up to the Eighteenth Century," *Journal of the Warburg and Courtauld Institutes* 21 (1958): 44–62, plate 8f; Georges Duplessis, *Essai Bibliographice sur les Différentes Éditions des Œuvres d'Ovid Ornées de Planches Publiées aux XVe et XVIe Siècles* (Paris, 1889), 17, 23–24; numbers 17, 59, 62.

45. *Works of Campion*, 255. See also the animation of statues in Francis Beaumont's *Masque of the Inner Temple* (1613).

46. Prunières, *Le Ballet de Cour*, 149; Lacroix, ed., *Ballets et Mascarades*, 2:3–4.

47. On the development of the myth and its various versions, see Raggio, "The Myth of Prometheus"; Raymond Trousson, *Le Thème de Prométheé dans la Littérature Européenne*, 2 vols. (Geneva: Droz, 1964), 1:85–141; Carl Kerényi, *Prometheus: Archetypal Image of Human Existence*, trans. Ralph Manheim (1963; Princeton, N. J.: Princeton University Press, 1997).

48. *Works of Campion*, 252.

49. *Natalis Comitis Mythologiæ sive Explicationum Fabularum*

Libri X (Venice, 1581), 6.20. Thanks to Jackson Bryce for making sense of my attempt to translate this passage.

50. George Sandys, *Ovid's Metamorphosis Englished, Mythologiz'd, and Represented in Figures,* ed. Karl K. Hulley and Stanley T. Vandersall (Lincoln, Nebr.: University of Nebraska Press, 1970), 62.

51. S. K. Heninger, Jr., *A Handbook of Renaissance Meteorology* (Durham, N. C.: Duke University Press, 1960), 37–46.

52. Heninger, *Handbook,* 45–46, 73–74, 96–97.

53. Plato, *Timaeus,* 41c–e; cf. Marsilio Ficino, *De Amore,* 4.4.

54. J. C. Eade, *The Forgotten Sky: A Guide to Astrology in English Literature* (Oxford: Clarendon Press, 1984), 66; Marsilio Ficino, *De Amore,* 5.8; Marsilio Ficino, *Three Books on Life,* ed. and trans. Carol V. Kaske and John R. Clark (Binghamton, N. Y.: Medieval & Renaissance Texts & Studies, 1989), 270–71, 292–93 (3.6, 11); George Chapman, *Andromeda Liberata,* lines 298–344; *The Poems of George Chapman,* ed. Phyllis Brooks Bartlett (New York: MLA; London: Oxford UP, 1941), 316–17; Edgar Wind, *Pagan Mysteries in the Renaissance,* rev. ed. (New York and London: Norton, 1968), 85–96; Raymond B. Waddington, *The Mind's Empire: Myth and Form in George Chapman's Narrative Poems* (Baltimore and London: Johns Hopkins University Press, 1974), 201–03.

55. Leone Ebreo, *The Philosophy of Love (Dialoghi d'Amore),* trans. F. Friedberg-Seeley and Jean H. Barnes (London: Soncino, 1937), 170, 175–76.

56. Apollonius Rhodius, *Argonautica,* 1.23–31; Ovid, *Metamorphoses,* 10.86–144.

57. Eyewitness accounts of the masque note that it opened with a dance of animals orchestrated by Orpheus and featuring a camel, a bear, and a hound; Andrew J. Sabol, ed., *A Score for* The Lords' Masque *by Thomas Campion* (Hanover and London: University Press of New England, 1993), 24–25, 326–27.

58. *Natalis Comitis Mythologiæ,* 6.20; Bernardus Silvestris, *Commentary on the First Six Books of Virgil's* Aeneid, trans. and ed. Earl G. Schreiber and Thomas E. Maresca (Lincoln, Nebr., and London: University of Nebraska Press, 1979), 76–77. On the common conflation of the Titans and the Giants, see DeWitt T. Starnes and Ernest William Talbert, *Classical Myth and Legend in Renaissance Dictionaries: A Study of Renaissance Dictionaries in their Relation to the Classical Learning of Contemporary English Writers* (Chapel Hill: University of North Carolina Press, 1955), 154–58.

59. *Natalis Comitis Mythologiæ,* 4.5.

60. *Omnia Andreæ Alciati V. C. Emblemata* (Antwerp, 1573), 93–95; number 22.

61. Sandys, *Ovid's Metamorphosis Englished,* 250.

62. See Raggio, "The Myth of Prometheus"; Trousson, *Le Thème de Prométheé*, 1:85–141; *Boccaccio on Poetry*, trans. Charles G. Osgood (Princeton, N. J.: Princeton University Press, 1930), xxiv–xxv; *Natalis Comitis Mythologiæ*, 4.6; Francis Bacon, *De Sapientia Veterum*, chapter 26; Charles W. Lemmi, *The Classic Deities in Bacon: A Study in Mythological Symbolism* (Baltimore: Johns Hopkins University Press, 1933), 128–40; Starnes and Talbert, *Classical Myth and Legend*, 154–58.

63. Sandys, *Ovid's Metamorphosis Englished*, 58.

64. Sandys, *Ovid's Metamorphosis Englished*, 61.

65. This political interpretation may be paralleled in other writings of the period: cf. George Chapman, *The Tragedy of Charles Duke of Byron*, 5.3.42–50, ed. John B. Gabel, in *The Plays of George Chapman. The Tragedies with Sir Gyles Goosecappe: A Critical Edition*, gen. ed. Allan Holaday (Cambridge: Brewer, 1987); Heninger, *Handbook*, 184–85.

66. On the intellectual background of this celebration of the inseparability of motion, dance, music, and love, see Gretchen Ludke Finney, *Musical Backgrounds for English Literature: 1580–1650* (New Brunswick, N. J.: Rutgers University Press, [1962]), 1–139.

67. Andrew J. Sabol, ed., *Four Hundred Songs and Dances from the Stuart Masque* (Providence, R. I.: Brown University Press, 1978), 9–12.

68. Jean Beaulieu to William Trumbull, 11/21 January 1620/21; BL, Trumbull Correspondence, MS VII, number 2.

69. On the distinction between ante- and anti-masque, see Welsford, *The Court Masque*, 184, 190–91.

70. Orgel, *The Jonsonian Masque*, 86.

71. Jennifer Stead, "Bowers of Bliss: The Banquet Setting," in C. Anne Wilson, ed., *"Banquetting Stuffe": The Fare and Social Background of the Tudor and Stuart Banquet* (Edinburgh: Edinburgh University Press, 1991), 115–57 (148); *Ben Jonson*, 7:698 (*Neptune's Triumph*, lines 494–95).

72. S. K. Heninger, Jr., *Touches of Sweet Harmony: Pythagorean Cosmology and Renaissance Poetics* (San Marino, Calif.: Huntington Library, 1974), 150–51.

73. Edmund Spenser, *The Faerie Queene*, 2.9.22; Alastair Fowler, *Spenser and the Numbers of Time* (New York: Barnes & Noble, 1964), 55–56, 273–74; *Works of Campion*, 213, note 13.

74. Butler, "Jonson's *News from the New World*," 164–65; *Ben Jonson*, 2:314; Ben Jonson, *Complete Masques*, 5.

75. *Ben Jonson*, 7:423.

76. Jonson, *Complete Masques*, 26.

77. Lacroix, ed., *Ballets et Mascarades*, 3:47.

78. See also Jonson's *News from the New World* (1620), lines 320–62, in which the monarch is figured as the source of light and motion (*Ben Jonson*, 7:523–24); Vaughan Hart, *Art and Magic in the Court of the Stuarts* (London and New York: Routledge, 1994), 155–59; Meagher, *Method and Meaning in Jonson's Masques*, chapter 5 (107–24); cf. the manner in which the royal gaze reanimates 12 knights turned into statues by the enchantress Alcina in the *Ballet de Monseigneur le duc de Vendome* (1610); Lacroix, ed., *Ballets et Mascarades*, 1:204, 261. The traditional assumption that the king's politics were absolutist has been challenged by Glenn Burgess, *Absolute Monarchy and the Stuart Constitution* (New Haven and London: Yale University Press, 1996), 40–43. But see also J. P. Sommerville, "James I and the divine right of kings: English politics and continental theory," and Paul Christianson, "Royal and parliamentary voices on the ancient constitution, c. 1604–1621," in Linda Levy Peck, ed., *The Mental World of the Jacobean Court* (Cambridge: Cambridge University Press, 1991), 55–70, 71–95.

79. Ficino, *De Amore*, 1.4.

80. The gustatory and tactile imagery that laces his speech registers his sensual depravity: see, for example, "Make temperance drunke," "Binde truth apprentise" (lines 71–72).

81. *De Amore*, 1.4.

82. Ficino, *De Amore*, 6.6, 7.10; Michael J. B. Allen, *The Platonism of Marsilio Ficino: A Study of His* Phaedrus *Commentary, Its Sources and Genesis* (Berkeley, Los Angeles, and London: University of California Press, 1984), 56–57, 191.

83. On the difficulty of the soul's descent, see Allen, *The Platonism of Marsilio Ficino*, 165–84.

84. Plato, **Phaedrus, 255c**;   *Marsilio Ficino and the Phaedran Charioteer*, ed. and trans. Michael J. B. Allen (Berkeley, Los Angeles, and London: University of California Press, 1981), 188; Allen, *The Platonism of Marsilio Ficino*, 195.

85. Plato, *Phaedrus*, 245c–246a; *Marsilio Ficino and the Phaedran Charioteer*, 86–97.

86. D. P. Walker, *Spiritual and Demonic Magic from Ficino to Campanella* (London: Warburg Institute, 1958), 3–24; Ficino, *Three Books on Life*.

87. Frances A. Yates, *Astraea: The Imperial Theme in the Sixteenth Century* (London and New York: RKP, 1975), 159–62.

88. Yates advanced this view of the Stuart masque in *Theatre of the World* (London and New York: RKP, 1969), 86; Douglas Brooks-Davies elaborated on it in *The Mercurian Monarch: Magical Politics from Spenser to Pope* (Manchester: Manchester University Press, 1983), chapter 2 (85–123); and Vaughan Hart reiterated it almost ver-

batim in *Art and Magic in the Court of the Stuarts*, 187 (cf. 17, 20).

89. *The Illusion of Power: Political Theater in the English Renaissance* (Berkeley, Los Angeles, and London: University of California Press, 1975), 55–58; cf. Walker, *Spiritual and Demonic Magic*, 120.

90. William D. Stahlman and Owen Gingerich, *Solar and Planetary Longitudes for Years –2500 to +2000 by 10-Day Intervals* (Madison: University of Wisconsin Press, 1963), 504; Eade, *The Forgotten Sky*, 61.

91. Ficino, *Three Books on Life*, 248 (3.1), 296 (3.11).

92. Orgel, *The Jonsonian Masque*, 99.

93. Canova-Green, 338–40; Frances A. Yates, *The French Academies of the Sixteenth Century* (London: Warburg Institute, 1947), 191. Boisrobert later employed the parallel of Titans and Huguenots in his *Grande Ballet de la Reyne* of 1623 (Lacroix, ed., *Ballets et Mascarades*, 2:353), as did Malherbe, in his ode "Pour le Roi allant châtier le rébellion Rochelois et chasser les Anglais" of 1627 (*Œuvres*, 158–63)—both men were, incidentally, known personally to Doncaster (see above, chapter 1: "Viscount Doncaster and his Magnificent Entertainments"). Théophile de Viau, who had accompanied Cadenet's embassy, alluded to the fall of the Giants in a *ballet de cour* performed shortly after his return to Paris (18 February 1621); *Œuvres Poétiques*, ed. Guido Saba (Paris: Garnier, 1990), v, 173.

94. *Ben Jonson*, 7:427.

95. On the popular representation of the worthies in English art and literature of this period, see Horst Schroeder, *Der Topos der Nine Worthies in Literatur und bildener Kunst* (Göttingen: Vandenhoeck and Ruprecht, 1971), 352–62. Their tendentiousness in the period 1619–21 is suggested by their appearance in Middleton's *Inner Temple Masque, or Masque of Heroes* (1619), in his and Rowley's *Courtly Masque* (which failed to receive a court performance), and also, perhaps, by their appearance in a civic procession planned at Chester in the summer of 1621 which did not, in the end, take place; BL, Harleian ms 2057 (Randall Holmes, Cheshire Collections), fol. 36r (cited by John L. Nevinson, "A Show of the Nine Worthies," *Shakespeare Quarterly* 14 (1963): 103–07 (105)).

96. Lacroix, ed., *Ballets et Mascarades*, 2:101–19; McGowan, *L'Art du Ballet de Cour*, 101–31, 179–81.

97. Barbara Lewalski suggests that Queen Anne's adoption of the role of Pallas in Daniel's *Vision of the Twelve Goddesses* (1604) may have involved some such dimension; *Writing Women in Jacobean England* (Cambridge, Mass., and London: Harvard University Press, 1993), 30.

98. On the iconographic expressions of James's pacifism, see D. J. Gordon, "Rubens and the Whitehall Ceiling," in *The Renaissance*

Imagination, ed. Orgel, 24–50 (41–49); Parry, *The Golden Age Restor'd,* 21–37; and Jonathan Goldberg, *James I and the Politics of Literature: Jonson, Shakespeare, Donne, and their Contemporaries* (Baltimore and London: Johns Hopkins University Press, 1983; Stanford: Stanford University Press, 1989), 43.

99. On Holles, see my "Who Danced in *The Essex House Masque* (1621)?," and on Blount, rumored to have been killed in the Low Countries in the summer of 1622, see *The Diary of Walter Yonge,* ed. George Roberts, Camden Society 41 (London, 1848), 64.

100. Marsilio Ficino, *De Amore,* 7.16; quoted from *Commentary on Plato's Symposium on Love,* trans. Sears Jayne (Dallas: Spring, 1985), 172.

101. Robert Zaller, *The Parliament of 1621: A Study in Constitutional Conflict* (Berkeley: University of California Press, 1971), 18–19; Goldberg, *James I and the Politics of Literature,* 65–85.

102. *Stuart Royal Proclamations,* 1:495–96; number 208.

103. The trope is rather similar to Jonson's presentation of the masquers as superlunary creatures, beyond the vulgar scrutiny of the newsmakers, in *News from the New World.*

104. Raylor, "Who Danced in *The Essex House Masque* (1621)?"

105. BL, Harleian MS 6103, fols. 3v, 4r.

106. Portal, "The Academ Roial of King James I," 207–08. Doncaster may have known Bolton himself, since he appears to have been employed on court business at this time. On 8 January 1620/21 an "Edwarde Bolton" was paid for bringing in letters from Sir Dudley Carleton, then Ambassador at the Hague; PRO E 351/544, fol. 133v.

107. Lockyer, *Buckingham,* 59–60.

108. Knowles, "Change Partners and Dance." If this was in fact the "running masque" hosted by Doncaster in the previous winter, the appearance of an antimasque of giants in Doncaster's masque of 1621 forms a nice bridge between the two events.

109. Knowles, "Change Partners and Dance."

110. Quoted from Knowles, "The 'Running Masque' Recovered?"

111. Knowles, "Change Partners and Dance"; Butler, "Jonson's *News from the New World,*" 160–61.

112. On the date of *Pan's Anniversary,* see Butler, "Ben Jonson's *Pan's Anniversary.*"

113. "Ben Jonson's *Pan's Anniversary.*"

114. Chamberlain, 2:333.

115. Leah S. Marcus, *The Politics of Mirth: Jonson, Herrick, Milton, Marvell, and the Defense of Old Holiday Pastimes* (Chicago and London: University of Chicago Press, 1986), 114–15; James Knowles, "Critical Introduction" to the *Inner Temple Masque, or Masque of Heroes* (1619), from the forthcoming Oxford edition of Middleton.

116. Carter, *Secret Diplomacy*, 211–12. Cadenet was clearly impressed by his reception in England; PRO, SP 78/69, fols. 4r, 37r; SP 84/99, fol. 95r.

117. British Library, Harleian MS 1581, fol. 17v. See also Chamberlain, 2:339.

118. Schreiber, 35–36; Schreiber, *The Political Career of Sir Robert Naunton*, 68–84; Butler, "Ben Jonson's *Pan's Anniversary*," 389, note 38; PRO, SP 84/99, fol. 4r; BL, Trumbull Correspondence, MS VII, number 2.

119. *CSPVen. 1619–1621*, 533–34.

120. *Mémoires Inédits du Comte Leveneur de Tillières*, 31; quoted in Canova-Green, 43.

121. Chamberlain, 2:432.

122. Zaller, *The Parliament of 1621*, 37, *et passim*; Conrad Russell, *Parliaments and English Politics 1621–1629* (Oxford: Oxford University Press, 1979), 85–144; Adams, "Foreign Policy and the Parliaments of 1621 and 1624," 159–64.

123. The scheme did not die completely, however: a similar academy, the *Musaeum Minervae*, was established by Sir Francis Kynaston in 1635; G. H. Turnbull, "Samuel Hartlib's Connection with Sir Francis Kynaston's 'Musaeum Minervae,'" *Notes & Queries* 197 (1952): 33–37.

124. *Ben Jonson*, 7:615 (lines 1475–78).

125. *Ben Jonson*, 2:315; Dale J. B. Randall, *Jonson's Gypsies Unmasked: Background and Theme of* The Gypsies Metamorphos'd (Durham, N. C.: Duke University Press, 1975), 143–52.

126. On the response to Campion, see David Lindley, "Embarrassing Ben: The Masques for Francis Howard," *English Literary Renaissance* 16 (1986): 343–59; on that to White, see Robert C. Evans, *Jonson and the Contexts of His Time* (Lewisburg: Bucknell University Press; London and Toronto: Associated University Presses, 1994), 95–115.

127. McGee and Meagher, "Preliminary Checklist," 115, 121. See also Knowles, "Change Partners and Dance"; John Orrell, "Buckingham's Patronage of the Dramatic Arts: The Crowe Accounts," *Records of the Early English Drama Newsletter* 2 (1980): 8–17.

Notes to Chapter Three

1. See, for instance, Jonson's description of the Theobalds entertainment of 1607 (*Ben Jonson*, 7:155) and Jones's sketches for similar scenes; Orgel and Strong, numbers 13–14.

2. *Ben Jonson*, 7:453–44 (lines 1–28).

3. Allan H. Gilbert, *Symbolic Persons in the Masques of Ben*

Jonson (Durham, N. C.: Duke University Press, 1948), 80–82.

4. Gilbert, *Symbolic Persons*, 183.

5. Orgel and Strong, number 105. On the appearance of animals in contemporary pageants and masques, see Wickham, *Early English Stages 1300–1660*, 2.1, 228–29; Nicoll, *Stuart Masques*, 205–6.

6. My suggestion in "The Design and Authorship of *The Essex House Masque*," 228, that the mines were invited onto the stage to dance was, I now think, mistaken.

7. For an explanation of this effect, see Nicoll, *Stuart Masques*, 76–77.

8. Prunières, *Le Ballet de Cour*, 149.

9. The classical notion that they had serpents for legs was not generally incorporated into Renaissance iconography: see, for example, the "Sala dei Giganti" in the Palazzo del Te at Mantua; Egon Verheyen, *The Palazzo del Te in Mantua: Images of Love and Politics* (Baltimore and London: Johns Hopkins University Press, 1977), plates 73–76; Arthur Henkel and Albert Schöne, *Emblemata* (Stuttgart: Metzersche, 1967), 1711–12.

10. See, for instance, the giant sketched by Jones for *Britannia Triumphans*; Orgel and Strong, numbers 372, 375.

11. See Horst Schroeder, "The Mural Paintings of the Nine Worthies at Amersham," *Archaeological Journal* 138 (1981): 241–47.

12. The civic pageant planned at Chester in the summer of 1621 was to have depicted them "in Compleat Armor with Crownes of gould on theire heads every on having his esqs to beare before him his sheild and penon of Armes, dressed according as there lords where accostomed to be; 3 Issaralits, 3 Infidels, 3 Christians &c."; Randall Holmes, Cheshire Collections, BL, Harleian MS 2057, fol. 36r.

13. On the used of the traverse, see Nicoll, *Stuart Masques*, 39.

14. On the background to and development of Jones's employment of scenes of this type, see Peacock, *Stage Designs*, 166–69.

15. Orgel and Strong, number 114.

16. Orgel and Strong, numbers 60–63.

17. See, for example, Bernardo Buontalenti's drawings for the mountain of Hamadryads in the second of the Florentine *intermedi* of 1589—reprinted in A. M. Nagler, *Theatre Festivals of the Medici, 1539–1637* (New Haven and London: Yale University Press, 1964), figures 48–49; and a sketch for the French *Ballet de la délivrance de Renaud* (1617), Bibliothèque Nationale, Paris: Prints, Est., Q.b.1617; reprinted in McGowan, *L'Art du Ballet de Cour*, plate IX; see also, Peacock, *Stage Designs*, plate 93.

18. See Glynne Wickham, *Early English Stages 1300–1600, Vol. 1: 1300–1576*, 2d ed. (London and Henley: RKP; New York: Columbia

University Press, 1980), 42, 220, 224–25; Wickham, *Early English Stages*, 2.1, 288; Orgel and Strong, number 13 (a mount designed for an entertainment at Hatfield House, 1608); Nagler, *Theatre Festivals*, figures 34–35 (a mount and cave designed for a barriers of 1579).

19. Nicoll, *Stuart Masques*, 67–69; Orgel and Strong, 1:17–19.

20. *Essayes or Councels, Civill and Morall*, ed. Michael Kiernan (Oxford: Clarendon Press, 1985), 117.

21. *Pratica di Fabricar Scene e Machine ne' Teatri* (1638), 2.24–26; trans. John H. McDowell, in Barnard Hewitt, ed., *The Renaissance Stage: Documents of Serlio, Sabbattini and Furttenbach* (Coral Gables: University of Miami Press, 1958), 37–177 (128–30; figure 60). The method consisted of using a wooden pole to raise a painted cloth in front of an actor.

22. In a note to the printed text of the masque, Campion complains that the painter, having demonstrated the operation of the trees to curious visitors during the day, had neglected to reattach them to the engine; *Works of Campion*, 222, note 44.

23. *Works of Campion*, 254; Nicoll, *Stuart Masques*, 76–77. It is perhaps worth recalling that Doncaster had danced in *The Lords' Masque*; *Works of Campion*, 284; Orgel and Strong, 1:241.

Notes to Chapter Four

1. D. J. Gordon, "Poet and Architect: The Intellectual Setting of the Quarrel between Ben Jonson and Inigo Jones," in *The Renaissance Imagination*, ed. Orgel, 77–101.

2. Compare, for instance, Jonson's account of the genesis of *The Masque of Blackness* in Queen Anne's desire to appear at the Twelfth Night festivities in black face, an explanatory fable for which he was to invent; *Ben Jonson*, 7:169 (lines 21–22).

3. Glynne Wickham, *Early English Stages*, 2.1, 242–44.

4. *Ben Jonson*, 7:454 (lines 27–28).

5. I have previously investigated this topic in "The Design and Authorship of *The Essex House Masque*"; my conclusions here are, however, rather different from those I reached there.

6. *The Poems and Masques of Aurelian Townshend*, ed. Cedric C. Brown (Reading: Whiteknights Press, 1983), 75.

7. John Peacock, "Inigo Jones and the Arundel Marbles," *Journal of Medieval and Renaissance Studies* 16 (1986): 75–90; Peacock, *Stage Designs*, 23.

8. Orgel and Strong, 1:403 (number 146).

9. *Ben Jonson*, 8:405 (lines 86–90).

10. *Ben Jonson*, 11:154; Ben Jonson, *Poems*, ed. Ian Donaldson (London: Oxford University Press, 1975), 324.

11. *Ben Jonson*, 8:406 (lines 98–99).

12. Orgel and Strong, numbers 100, 102. Orgel and Strong associate these sketches with the masque of 1619, which Jonson was not responsible for devising; 1:299.

13. On the chronology of the dispute, see Gordon, "Poet and Architect."

14. On the dangers of impressionism in matters of attribution, see S. Schoenbaum, *Internal Evidence and Elizabethan Dramatic Authorship: An Essay in Literary History and Method* (Evanston: Northwestern University Press, 1966).

15. Peacock, *Stage Designs*, chapter 5 (158–207); Peacock notes, however, that the absence of drawings from the period 1611–20 makes it difficult to generalize about the development of Jones's style in that decade.

16. Schedule of Creditors of the first earl of Carlisle, House of Lords Record Office, Main Papers, 18 January 1640/41.

17. David Bergeron, *English Civic Pageantry 1558–1642* (London: Arnold, 1971), 151, 250; Edward Croft-Murray, *Decorative Painting in England 1537–1837*, vol. 1: *Early Tudor to Sir James Thornhill* (London: Country Life, 1962), 194.

18. Orgel and Strong, 1:37, 180.

19. I have surveyed the evidence for rejecting most of those poets who are known to have moved in Doncaster's orbit in my article, "The Design and Authorship of *The Essex House Masque*."

20. I made such a case in "The Design and Authorship of *The Essex House Masque*," 226–28.

21. "The Design and Authorship of *The Essex House Masque*," 223.

22. *Ben Jonson* 1:133.

23. Martin Butler, "Courtly Negotiations: The Stuart Court Masque and Political Culture 1603–42" (work in progress), Appendix C.

24. See Raymond B. Waddington, *The Mind's Empire*, 21–30.

25. *The Poems of George Chapman*, ed. Phyllis Brooks Bartlett, 22, 388. All quotations from Chapman's English poems are taken from this edition; they are cited, where appropriate, by line number only.

26. *George Chapman's Minor Translations: A Critical Edition of his Renderings of Musaeus, Hesiod and Juvenal*, ed. Richard Corballis, Salzburg Studies in English Literature: Jacobean Drama Studies, 98 (Salzburg: Salzburg University, 1984), 58 (note 22). The

footnote refers the reader to Bacon's interpretation of the myth in *De Sapientia Veterum* (1609), chapter 26, despite the fact that Bacon's reading does not corroborate the version of the myth here adumbrated. The Prometheus of *The Essex House Masque* is closer to the creative artist of the "Hymnus" and the dedicatory poem than to the thief of *The Georgicks*.

27. *The Jonsonian Masque*, 102.

28. *Ben Jonson and Elizabethan Music* (1929; reprint, New York: Da Capo, 1965), 119.

29. Jack E. Reese, "Unity in Chapman's *Masque of the Middle Temple and Lincoln's Inn*," *Studies in English Literature* 4 (1964): 291–305 (292).

30. "Hymnus in Noctem," lines 123–200. I am here indebted to Waddington, *The Mind's Empire*, 106.

31. Heninger, *Handbook*, 183–99; Alastair Fowler, *Triumphal Forms: Structural Patterns in Elizabethan Poetry* (Cambridge: Cambridge University Press, 1971), 140–46, 208–14.

32. D. J. Gordon has demonstrated Chapman's metaphoric employment of the comet as a celestial phenomenon in *Hero and Leander*, 5.481–90, in "The Renaissance Poet as Classicist: Chapman's *Hero and Leander*," in *The Renaissance Imagination*, ed. Orgel, 102–33 (107–08); cf. *Essex House Masque*, line 170 and note.

33. Donald W. Foster, *Elegy by W. S.: A Study in Attribution* (Newark, Del.: University of Delaware Press; London and Toronto: Associated University Presses, 1989), 148; table 1.19. Foster has examined Chapman's three elegies from this period: *An Epicede on Henry Prince of Wales, Eugenia*, and "To the Immortall Memorie of . . . Henry, Prince of Wales," from *The Whole Works of Homer* (295).

34. In calculating this rate, I have tried to adhere to Foster's method (that of counting only lines that do not, by our standards, require end-punctuation, and that are not followed by parentheses); *Elegy by W. S.*, 83–84. Of course, Foster and I may differ in our judgment of such matters.

35. *Elegy by W. S.*, 84–86; table 1.1.

36. *Elegy by W. S.*, 84.

37. Phyllis Bartlett, ed., *The Poems of George Chapman*, 11–15.

38. See, for example: "refine" | "divine" (*Essex House Masque*, lines 178–79; "Hymnus in Cynthiam," lines 154–55); and "can" | "man"; *Essex House Masque*, lines 174–75; "To the Right Worthily Honored, Robert Earle of Sommerset, &c."—the dedicatory poem to *Andromeda Liberata* (1614)—lines 64–65.

39. There is, in any case, some dispute about the status of a number of supposed Chapman holographs; for a summary (with

illustration) see Peter Beal, comp., *Index of English Literary Manuscripts, Vol. 1: 1450–1625*, 2 vols. (London and New York: Mansell, 1980), 1:191–93. For a full investigation, see L. A. Cummings, *Geo: Chapman his Crowne & Conclusion: A Study of his Handwriting*, Salzburg Studies in English Literature: Elizabethan and Renaissance Studies, 106 (Salzburg: University of Salzburg, 1989).

40. G. Blakemore Evans, "Textual Introduction" to *The Memorable Masque*, in *The Plays of George Chapman: The Comedies: A Critical Edition*, gen. ed., Allan Holaday (Urbana, Chicago, and London: University of Illinois Press, 1970), 560.

41. Blakemore Evans attributes the correction of these spellings to compositorial interference, rather than authorial correction (560).

42. Welsford, *The Court Masque*, 184, 190, 197, 211; *Poems and Masques of Aurelian Townshend*, 109. On the attribution of the *Masque of the Twelve Months* to Chapman, see Butler, "Courtly Negotiations," Appendix C.

43. Cyrus Hoy, "The Shares of Fletcher and His Collaborators in the Beaumont and Fletcher Canon (VI)," *Studies in Bibliography* 14 (1961): 45–68 (61–64).

44. On this problem in Hoy's work, see Jonathan Hope, *The Authorship of Shakespeare's Plays: A Socio-Linguistic Study* (Cambridge: Cambridge University Press, 1994), 67–76.

45. Hope, *The Authorship of Shakespeare's Plays*, 15–17.

46. Hope, *The Authorship of Shakespeare's Plays*, 14–15. Charles Barber, *Early Modern English* (London: Deutsch, 1976), 265, claims that the use of periphrastic "do" in this period marks a "literary" as opposed to a colloquial style (cited by Hope, 14). The need for metrical "fillers" might also contribute to increased rates of auxiliary usage in verse.

47. In calculating these figures I have attempted to follow the counting method outlined by Hope, *The Authorship of Shakespeare's Plays*, 15–17.

48. *Chapman's Homer*, ed. Allardyce Nicoll, 2 vols. (New York: Pantheon, 1956), 2:539. The publication date of Chapman's translation of the lesser Homerica is unknown, but was certainly after 1622: see *Poems of Chapman*, 487.

49. See also, "Love, is Natures second sunne, | Causing a spring of vertues where he shines"; Chapman, *All Fools* (1605), 1.1.97–98 (*The Comedies*, gen. ed., Holaday).

50. In searching for this phrase I have made use of *English Poetry Full-Text Database* and *English Drama: The Full-Text Database*, published by Chadwyck-Healey and available on line through *Literature Online*: http://www.chadwyck.com/.

51. *The Plays & Poems of Robert Greene*, ed. J. Churton Collins,

2 vols. (Oxford: Clarendon Press, 1905), 1:246; *Works of Middleton,* 6:383 (1.2.84–85). Middleton's usage does not appear to be close enough to that of the masque to be significant. Orthographic evidence against his authorship of the masque was reviewed in my article "The Design and Authorship of *The Essex House Masque,*" 223.

52. Schoenbaum, *Internal Evidence,* 189–93.

53. C. J. Sisson and Robert Butman, "George Chapman, 1612–22: Some New Facts," *Modern Language Review* 46 (1951): 185–90.

54. Chapman's legal problems had a financial base, and his penury was notorious among his contemporaries; Sisson and Butman, "George Chapman," 185, 190.

55. Edmund Bolton, *Hypercritica,* in J. E. Spingarn, ed., *Critical Essays of the Seventeenth Century,* 3 vols. (Oxford: Clarendon Press, 1908–09), 1:110; Portal, "Academ Roial," 198, 207.

56. A. R. Braunmuller, "Robert Carr, Earl of Somerset, as collector and patron," in Peck, ed., *The Mental World of the Jacobean Court,* 230–50 (240–46).

57. Schreiber, 11–13.

58. Chamberlain, 2:19, 77.

59. *Poems of Chapman,* 19; *Chapman's Homer,* 1:16; John W. Shirley, *Thomas Harriot: A Biography* (Oxford: Clarendon Press, 1983), 65–68, 359–60, 373–76.

60. Chapman's *Iliads* appears among a list of books sent by Northumberland from the Tower to Syon House in December 1614; Alnwick Castle MS W.II, fol. 1r. A copy of *The Whole Works of Homer* (London, [1616?]), with verses "ad famam" inscribed—though not in the author's hand—between the preface and the main text, survives in the library of the duke of Northumberland at Alnwick Castle, Northumberland (shelfmark 29/5). I am grateful to Dr Stephen Clucas, of Birkbeck College, London, for this information about Northumberland's books.

61. G. R. Batho, *Thomas Harriot and the Northumberland Household,* Durham Thomas Harriot Society, Occasional Paper 1 (1983): 12.

62. Chamberlain, 2:318–19; Shirley, *Harriot,* 291, 365.

63. Schreiber, 20–21, 38.

64. Chapman's political affiliations are elegantly summarized by A. R. Braunmuller in *Natural Fictions: George Chapman's Major Tragedies* (Newark, Del.: University of Delaware Press; London and Toronto: Associated University Presses, 1992), 19–24, 132–42; the breakdown of relations between him and Jonson is analyzed in *Ben Jonson,* 10:692–97.

65. Title page reproduced in *The Comedies,* gen. ed., Holaday, 563.

66. *Chapman's Minor Translations*, 1. The possibility that Jones was the designer of the Homer title page is raised by Margery Corbett and Ronald Lightbown in *The Comely Frontispience: The Emblematic Title-Page in England 1550–1660* (London, Henley, and Boston: RKP, 1979), 116.

67. *Ben Jonson*, 10:689–97.

Works Cited

This list contains those works to which specific reference is made, with the exception of standard reference works, works that may be consulted in any standard edition (e.g. the poetry of Shakespeare and Spenser), and classical texts. References to classical texts are keyed to the line numbers of the respective Loeb Classical Library editions.

Manuscripts

Great Britain

Alnwick Castle, Northumberland (Library of the duke of Northumberland). Shelfmark 29/5. George Chapman. Manuscript verses inscribed between the preface and the main text of *The Whole Works of Homer*. London, [1616?].

———. MS W.II, fol. 1r. Henry Percy, First earl of Northumberland. List of books sent from the Tower to Syon House in December 1614.

Bodleian Library, Oxford. MS Don. C. 24. Nicholas Oldisworth. "Recollection of Certain Scattered Poems" (1644).

British Library. Additional MS 7082. Letterbook of Edward Herbert.

———. Additional MS 12528. Transcript of the Account Book of Sir Sackville Crowe.

———. Egerton MSS 2592–97. Correspondence of James Hay, Viscount Doncaster.

———. Harleian MS 1581, fol. 17. Edward Herbert to George Villiers, marquess of Buckingham, 15 February 1621.

———. Harleian MS 2057. Randall Holmes. Cheshire Collections.

———. Harleian MS 6103. Edmund Bolton. Proposal for establishing an Academy of Honor (1620).

———. Lansdowne MSS 207 B, 207 E. Gervase Holles. Historical Collections.

———. Lansdowne MS 350, fols. 139–78. John Ford. "Linea Vitae. A Line of Life."

———. Royal MS 16E.XVIII. Marc de Mailliet. "Au Roy de la grande Bretaigne: ode" (1617).

———. (Uncatalogued). Trumbull Correspondence.

Hallward Library, University of Nottingham. Pw V 6. Gervase Holles. Memorials of the Holles Family.

House of Lords Record Office. Main Papers. 18 January 1640/41. Schedule of Creditors of the first earl of Carlisle.

Public Record Office, London. E 351/544. Accounts of William Uvedale, Treasurer of the King's Chamber.

———. PRO 31/3/54, fols. 145–448. Instructions for the embassy of maréchal de Cadenet. (Baschet Transcripts of Records in French Archives.)

———. SP 14/198/20. Marc de Mailliet. "A la lovange de Monsieur de Hay ode."

———. SP 78/66. State Papers, Jacobean.

———. SP 78/68. State Papers, Jacobean.

———. SP 78/69. State Papers, Jacobean.

———. SP 78/98. State Papers, Jacobean.

———. SP 84/99. State Papers, Jacobean.

U.S.A.

Houghton Library, Harvard University. Houghton MS Eng 686, fol. 20. "Upon the French Embassadours enterteinement in England at W. Hall Dec. 30 1620."

Printed Works

Adams, Simon. "Captain Thomas Gainsford, the 'Vox Spiritus' and the *Vox Populi.*" *Bulletin of the Institute of Historical Research* 49 (1976): 141–44.

———. "Foreign Policy and the Parliaments of 1621 and 1624." In Kevin Sharpe, ed., *Faction and Parliament: Essays on Early Stuart History*, 139–71. Oxford: Oxford University Press, 1978. Reprint, London and New York: Methuen, 1985.

———. "The Road to La Rochelle: English Foreign Policy and the Huguenots, 1610–1629." *Proceedings of the Huguenot Society of London* 22 (1975): 414–29.

Akrigg, G. P. V. *Jacobean Pageant or The Court of King James I.* Cambridge, Mass.: Harvard University Press, 1963.

Alciati, Andrea. *Omnia Andreæ Alciati V. C. Emblemata.* Antwerp, 1573.

Allen, Michael J. B. *The Platonism of Marsilio Ficino: A Study of His* Phaedrus *Commentary, Its Sources and Genesis.* Berkeley, Los Angeles, and London: University of California Press, 1984.

Aneau, Barthelemy. *Picta Poesis.* Lyons, 1552.

Ashton, Robert, ed. *James I by his Contemporaries.* London: Hutchinson, 1969.

Aubrey, John. *Brief Lives, chiefly of Contemporaries, set down by John Aubrey, between the Years 1669 & 1696.* Ed. Andrew Clark. 2 vols. Oxford, 1898.

Ayton, Robert. *Basia.* London, 1606.

———. *The English and Latin Poems of Sir Robert Ayton.* Ed. Charles B. Gullans. Scottish Text Society, 4th series, 1. Edinburgh, 1963.

Bacon, Francis. *De Sapientia Veterum.* London, 1609.

———. *Essayes or Councels, Civill and Morall.* Ed. Michael Kiernan. Oxford: Clarendon Press, 1985.

———. *The Works of Francis Bacon.* Ed. James Spedding, Robert Leslie Ellis, and Douglas Denon Heath. 14 vols. London, 1857–74.

Baïf, Jean Antoine de. *Euvres en Rime de Ian Antoine de Baif.* Ed. Ch. Marty-Laveaux. 5 vols. Paris, 1881–90.

Bald, R. C. *John Donne: A Life.* Oxford: Clarendon Press, 1970.

Barber, Charles. *Early Modern English*. London: Deutsch, 1976.

Bassompierre, François de. *Negociation du Mareschal de Bassompierre envoyé Ambassadeur Extraordinaire, en Angleterre . . . 1626*. Cologne, 1668.

Batho, G. R. *Thomas Harriot and the Northumberland Household*. Durham Thomas Harriot Society, Occasional Paper 1. 1983.

Beal, Peter, comp., *Index of English Literary Manuscripts, Vol. 1: 1450–1625*. 2 vols. London and New York: Mansell, 1980.

Bentley, Gerald Eades. *The Jacobean and Caroline Stage*. 7 vols. Oxford: Clarendon Press, 1941–68.

Bergeron, David. *English Civic Pageantry 1558–1642*. London: Arnold, 1971.

Boccaccio, Giovanni. *Boccaccio on Poetry*. Trans. Charles G. Osgood. Princeton, N. J.: Princeton University Press, 1930.

Bolton, Edmund. *Hypercritica*. In J. E. Spingarn, ed., *Critical Essays of the Seventeenth Century*, 3 vols. 1:82–115. Oxford: Clarendon Press, 1908–09.

Braunmuller, A. R. *Natural Fictions: George Chapman's Major Tragedies*. Newark, Del.: University of Delaware Press; London and Toronto: Associated University Presses, 1992.

———. "Robert Carr, Earl of Somerset, as collector and patron." In Linda Levy Peck, ed., *The Mental World of the Jacobean Court*, 230–50. Cambridge: Cambridge University Press, 1991.

Bromham, A. A., and Zara Bruzzi. *The Changeling and the Years of Crisis, 1619–1624: A Hieroglyph of England*. London and New York: Pinter, 1990.

Brooks-Davies, Douglas. *The Mercurian Monarch: Magical Politics from Spenser to Pope*. Manchester: Manchester University Press, 1983.

Burgess, Glenn. *Absolute Monarchy and the Stuart Constitution*. New Haven and London: Yale University Press, 1996.

Butler, Martin. "Courtly Negotiations: The Stuart Court Masque and Political Culture 1603–42." Work in progress.

———. "Ben Jonson's *Pan's Anniversary* and the Politics of Early Stuart Pastoral." *English Literary Renaissance* 22 (1992): 369–404.

———. "Jonson's *News from the New World*, the 'Running Masque', and the Season of 1619–20." *Medieval & Renaissance Drama in England* 6 (1993): 153–78.

————. "Politics and the Masque: *Salmacida Spolia.*" In Thomas Healy and Jonathan Sawday, eds., *Literature and the English Civil War*, 59–74. Cambridge: Cambridge University Press, 1990.

Calendar of State Papers, Domestic Series, of the Reign of James I., 1619–1623. Ed. Mary Anne Everett Green. London, 1858.

Calendar of State Papers and Manuscripts, Relating to English Affairs, Existing in the Archives and Collections of Venice. Vol. 16. *1619–1621.* Ed. Allen B. Hinds. London: HMSO, 1910.

Calendar of State Papers and Manuscripts, Relating to English Affairs, Existing in the Archives and Collections of Venice. Vol. 20. *1626–1628.* Ed. Allen B. Hinds. London: HMSO, 1914.

Campion, Thomas. *The Works of Thomas Campion.* Ed. Walter R. Davis. New York: Doubleday, 1967. Reprint, London: Faber, 1969.

Canova-Green, Marie-Claude. *La politique-spectacle au grand siècle: les rapports franco-anglais.* Paris, Seattle, and Tübingen: Biblio 17, 1993.

Carew, George. *Letters from George Carew to Sir Thomas Roe.* Ed. John Maclean. Camden Society 76. London, 1860.

Carew, Thomas. *The Poems of Thomas Carew with his Masque Coelum Britannicum.* Ed. Rhodes Dunlap. Oxford: Clarendon Press, 1949.

Carter, Charles Howard. *The Secret Diplomacy of the Hapsburgs, 1598–1625.* New York: Columbia University Press, 1964.

Chadwyck-Healey. *English Drama: The Full-Text Database. Literature Online*: http://www.chadwyck.com/.

————. *English Poetry Full-Text Database. Literature Online*: http://www.chadwyck.com/.

Chamberlain, John. *The Letters of John Chamberlain.* Ed. Norman Egbert McClure. Memoirs of the American Philosophical Society. Vol. 12. 2 vols. Philadelphia: American Philosophical Society, 1939.

Chapman, George. *Chapman's Homer.* Ed. Allardyce Nicoll. 2 vols. New York: Pantheon, 1956.

————. *George Chapman's Minor Translations: A Critical Edition of his Renderings of Musaeus, Hesiod and Juvenal.* Ed. Richard Corballis. Salzburg Studies in English Literature: Jacobean Drama Studies, 98. Salzburg: Salzburg University, 1984.

————. *The Plays of George Chapman. The Comedies: A Critical*

Edition. Gen ed. Allan Holaday. Urbana, Chicago, and London: University of Illinois Press, 1970.

———. *The Plays of George Chapman. The Tragedies with* Sir Gyles Goosecappe: *A Critical Edition.* Gen ed. Allan Holaday. Cambridge: Brewer, 1987.

———. *The Poems of George Chapman.* Ed. Phyllis Brooks Bartlett. New York and London: MLA, 1941.

———. *The Whole Works of Homer.* London, [1616?].

Christianson, Paul. "Royal and parliamentary voices on the ancient constitution, *c.* 1604–1621." In Linda Levy Peck, ed., *The Mental World of the Jacobean Court,* 71–95. Cambridge: Cambridge University Press, 1991.

Clarendon, Edward Hyde, earl of. *The History of the Rebellion and Civil Wars in England.* Ed. W. Dunn Macray. 6 vols. Oxford, 1888.

Comes, Natalis. *Natalis Comitis Mythologiæ sive Explicationum Fabularum Libri X.* Venice, 1581.

C[ooper], T[homas]. "Bolton or Boulton, Edmund (1575?-1633)." *Dictionary of National Biography.*

Corbett, Margery and Ronald Lightbown. *The Comely Frontispiece: The Emblematic Title-Page in England 1550–1660.* London, Henley, and Boston: RKP, 1979.

Corbett, Richard. *The Poems of Richard Corbett.* Ed. J. A. W. Bennett and H. R. Trevor-Roper. Oxford: Clarendon Press, 1955.

Craig, Alexander. *Poetical Recreations.* Edinburgh, 1609.

———. *Poetical Recreations.* Aberdeen, 1623.

———. *The Poetical Works of Alexander Craig of Rose-Craig 1604–1631.* Intro. David Laing. Glasgow, 1872.

Croft-Murray, Edward. *Decorative Painting in England 1537–1837.* Vol. 1: *Early Tudor to Sir James Thornhill.* London: Country Life, 1962.

Cummings, L. A. *Geo: Chapman his Crowne & Conclusion: A Study of his Handwriting,* Salzburg Studies in English Literature: Elizabethan and Renaissance Studies, 106. Salzburg: University of Salzburg, 1989.

Davies, John, of Hereford. *Bien Venu.* London, 1606.

D'Ewes, Simonds. *The Autobiography and Correspondence of Sir Simonds D'Ewes.* Ed. James Orchard Halliwell. 2 vols. London, 1845.

Doort, Abraham van der. "Abraham van der Doort's Catalogue of the Collections of Charles I." Ed. Oliver Millar. *The Walpole Society* 37 (1958–60 [1960]).

Duplessis, Georges. *Essai Bibliographice sur les Différentes Éditions des Œuvres d'Ovid Ornées de Planches Publiées aux XVe et XVIe Siècles.* Paris, 1889.

Eade, J. C. *The Forgotten Sky: A Guide to Astrology in English Literature.* Oxford: Clarendon Press, 1984.

Ebreo, Leone. *The Philosophy of Love (Dialoghi d'Amore).* Trans. F. Friedberg-Seeley and Jean H. Barnes. London: Soncino, 1937.

Elizabeth of Bohemia. *The Letters of Elizabeth Queen of Bohemia.* Comp. L. M. Baker. Intro. C. V. Wedgwood. London: Bodley Head, 1953.

Evans, Robert C. *Jonson and the Contexts of His Time.* Lewisburg: Bucknell University Press; London, and Toronto: Associated University Presses, 1994.

Evans, Willa McClung. *Ben Jonson and Elizabethan Music.* 1929. Reprint, New York: Da Capo, 1965.

Ficino, Marsilio. [*De Amore*]: *Commentary on Plato's Symposium on Love.* Trans. Sears Jayne. Dallas: Spring, 1985.

———. *Marsilio Ficino and the Phaedran Charioteer.* Ed. and trans. Michael J. B. Allen. Berkeley, Los Angeles, and London: University of California Press, 1981.

———. *Three Books on Life.* Ed. and trans. Carol V. Kaske and John R. Clark. Binghamton, N. Y.: Medieval & Renaissance Texts & Studies, 1989.

Finett, John. *Finetti Philoxenis.* London, 1656.

Finney, Gretchen Ludke. *Musical Backgrounds for English Literature: 1580–1650.* New Brunswick, N. J.: Rutgers University Press, 1962.

Ford, John. *The Nondramatic Works of John Ford.* Ed. L. E. Stock, Gilles P. Monsarrat, Judith M. Kennedy, and Dennis Danielson. Binghamton, N. Y.: Medieval & Renaissance Texts & Studies, 1991.

Foster, Donald W. *Elegy by W. S.: A Study in Attribution.* Newark, Del.: University of Delaware Press; London and Toronto: Associated University Presses, 1989.

Fowler, Alastair. *Spenser and the Numbers of Time.* New York: Barnes & Noble, 1964.

————. *Triumphal Forms: Structural Patterns in Elizabethan Poetry*. Cambridge: Cambridge University Press, 1971.

Fumerton, Patricia. *Cultural Aesthetics: Renaissance Life and the Practice of Cultural Ornament*. Chicago and London: University of Chicago Press, 1991.

Furniss, W. Todd. "Ben Jonson's Masques." In *Three Studies in the Renaissance*, 89–179. New Haven: Yale University Press, 1958.

Gainsford, Thomas. *Vox Spiritus, or Sir Walter Rawleigh's Ghost*. Exeter, England: The Rota, 1983.

Galilei, Galileo, et al. *The Controversy on the Comets of 1618*. Trans. Stillman Drake and C. D. O'Malley. Philadelphia: University of Pennsylvania Press, 1960.

Gardiner, Samuel Rawson. "Hay, James, first Earl of Carlisle, first Viscount Doncaster, and first Baron Hay (d. 1636)." *Dictionary of National Biography*.

————. *History of England from the Accession of James I. to the Outbreak of the Civil War 1603–42*. 10 vols. London, 1883–84.

————. *A History of England under the Duke of Buckingham and Charles I: 1625–1628*. 2 vols. London, 1875.

————, ed. *Letters and Other Documents Illustrating the Relations Between England and Germany at the Commencement of the Thirty Years' War*. Camden Society, 2d series, 98. London, 1868.

Gilbert, Allan H. *Symbolic Persons in the Masques of Ben Jonson*. Durham, N. C.: Duke University Press, 1948.

Goldberg, Jonathan. *James I and the Politics of Literature: Jonson, Shakespeare, Donne, and their Contemporaries*. Baltimore and London: Johns Hopkins University Press, 1983; Stanford: Stanford University Press, 1989.

G[oodwin], G[ordon]. "Holles, Gervase (1606–1675)." *Dictionary of National Biography*.

Gordon, D. J. *The Renaissance Imagination*, ed. Stephen Orgel. Berkeley, Los Angeles, and London: University of California Press, 1975.

————. "Poet and Architect: The Intellectual Setting of the Quarrel between Ben Jonson and Inigo Jones," 77–101.

————. "The Renaissance Poet as Classicist: Chapman's *Hero and Leander*," 102–33.

————. "Rubens and the Whitehall Ceiling," 24–50.

Goulding, R. W. "Gervase Holles, a great lover of antiquities." *Transactions of the Thoroton Society* 26 (1922): 36–70.

Graham-White, Anthony. *Punctuation and its Dramatic Value in Shakespearean Drama*. Newark, Del.: University of Delaware Press; London: Associated University Presses, 1995.

Greg, W. W. *A List of Masques, Pageants, &c.* London: Bibliographical Society, 1902.

Green, Mary Anne Everett. *Elizabeth, Electress Palatine and Queen of Bohemia*. Revised by S. C. Lomas. London: Methuen, 1909.

Greene, Robert. *The Plays & Poems of Robert Greene*. Ed. J. Churton Collins, 2 vols. Oxford: Clarendon Press, 1905.

Harris, John. "The Link between a Roman second-century sculptor, Van Dyck, Inigo Jones and Queen Henrietta Maria." *Burlington Magazine* 115 (1973): 526–30.

Hart, Vaughan. *Art and Magic in the Court of the Stuarts*. London and New York: Routledge, 1994.

Harvie, Ron. "A Present from 'Dear Dad'?: Van Dyck's *The Continence of Scipio*." *Apollo* 138 (1993): 224–26.

Haynes, D. E. L. *The Arundel Marbles*. Oxford: Ashmolean Museum, 1975.

———. "The Fawley Court Relief." *Apollo* 96 (1972): 6–10.

Heninger, S. K., Jr. *A Handbook of Renaissance Meteorology*. Durham, N. C.: Duke University Press, 1960.

———. *Touches of Sweet Harmony: Pythagorean Cosmology and Renaissance Poetics*. San Marino, Calif.: Huntington Library, 1974.

Henkel, Arthur and Albert Schöne. *Emblemata*. Stuttgart: Metzersche, 1967.

Hind, Arthur M. *Engraving in England in the Sixteenth & Seventeenth Centuries: A Descriptive Catalogue with Introductions, 2: The Reign of James I*. Cambridge: Cambridge University Press, 1955.

Historical Manuscripts Commission 75. *Report on the Manuscripts of the Most Honourable the Marquess of Downshire formerly at Easthampstead Park, Berkshire, 6: Papers of William Trumbull the Elder, September 1616—December 1618*. Ed. G. Dyfnallt Owen and Sonia P. Anderson. London: HMSO, 1995.

——— 9. *Salisbury (Cecil) Manuscripts, 24: Addenda 1605–1668*. Ed. G. Dyfnallt Owen. London: HMSO, 1976.

Holles, Gervase. *Memorials of the Holles Family 1493–1656*. Ed. A. C. Wood. Camden Society, 3d series, 55. London, 1937.

Holles, John. *The Letters of John Holles, 1587–1637*. Ed. P. R. Seddon. 3 vols. Thoroton Society Record Series 31, 35, and 36. Nottingham, 1975, 1983, and 1986.

Hope, Jonathan. *The Authorship of Shakespeare's Plays: A Socio-Linguistic Study*. Cambridge: Cambridge University Press, 1994.

House of Lords. *Journals of the House of Lords*. [n. p.: n. d.].

Howarth, David. *Lord Arundel and his Circle*. New Haven and London: Yale University Press, 1985.

Hoy, Cyrus. "The Shares of Fletcher and His Collaborators in the Beaumont and Fletcher Canon (VI)." *Studies in Bibliography* 14 (1961): 45–68.

Jacquot, Jean. "Le reine Henriette-Marie et l'influence française dans les spectacles à la cour de Charles Ier." 9e *Cahiers de l'association international des études françaises* (1957), 128–60.

James I. *The Kings Majesties Declaration to His Subjects Concerning lawfull Sports to be used*. London, 1618.

———. *The Poems of James VI. of Scotland*. Ed. James Craigie. 2 vols., Scottish Text Society, 3d series, 22 and 26. Edinburgh, 1955 and 1958.

Johnston, Arthur. *Epigrammata*. Aberdeen, 1632.

———. *Musæ Querulæ, de Regis in Scotiam Profectione*. London, 1633.

Jones, Inigo. *Inigo Jones on Palladio*. Ed. Bruce Allsopp. 2 vols. Newcastle upon Tyne: Oriel Press, 1970.

Jonson, Ben. *The Complete Masques*. Ed. Stephen Orgel. New Haven and London: Yale University Press, 1969.

———. *Ben Jonson*. Ed. C. H. Herford, Percy and Evelyn Simpson. 11 vols. Oxford: Clarendon Press, 1925–52.

———. *Poems*. Ed. Ian Donaldson. London: Oxford University Press, 1975.

Kerényi, Carl. *Prometheus: Archetypal Image of Human Existence*. Trans. Ralph Manheim. 1963; Princeton, N. J.: Princeton University Press, 1997.

Kingsford, Charles Lethbridge. "Essex House, formerly Leicester House and Exeter Inn." *Archaeologia* 73 (1923): 1–54.

Knowles, James. "Change Partners and Dance: A Newly Discovered Jacobean Masque." *Times Literary Supplement*. 9 August, 1991, 19.

———. "Critical Introduction" to the *Inner Temple Masque, or Masque of Heroes* (1619), from the forthcoming Oxford edition of Thomas Middleton's works.

———. "Marston, Skipwith and *The Entertainment at Ashby*." *English Manuscript Studies 1100–1700* 3 (1992): 137–92.

———. "The 'Running Masque' Recovered?: A Masque for the Marquess of Buckingham (c. 1619–21)," *English Manuscript Studies 1100–1700* 8 (1999).

Kunzle, David. "Van Dyck's *Continence of Scipio* as a Metaphor of Statecraft at the Early Stuart Court." In John Onians, ed., *Sight and Insight: Essays on Art and Culture in Honour of E. H. Gombrich at 85*, 168–89. London: Phaidon, 1994.

Kyd, Thomas. *The Spanish Tragedy*. Ed. Philip Edwards. London: Methuen, 1959.

Lacroix, Paul, ed. *Ballets et Mascarades de Cour de Henri III a Louis XIV*. 6 vols. Geneva and Turin, 1868–70.

Lancashire, Anne, ed. *The Second Maiden's Tragedy*. Manchester: Manchester University Press; Baltimore: Johns Hopkins University Press, 1978.

L[ee], S[idney]. "Blount, Lord Mountjoy, and Earl of Newport (1597–1666)." *Dictionary of National Biography*.

Leech, John. *Musæ Priores, sive Poematum Pars Prior*. London, 1620.

Lemmi, Charles W. *The Classic Deities in Bacon: A Study in Mythological Symbolism*. Baltimore: Johns Hopkins University Press, 1933.

Lewalski, Barbara Kiefer. *Writing Women in Jacobean England*. Cambridge, Mass., and London: Harvard University Press, 1993.

Lindley, David. "Embarrassing Ben: The Masques for Francis Howard." *English Literary Renaissance* 16 (1986): 343–59.

———. *Thomas Campion*. Leiden: Brill, 1989.

———. "Who paid for Campion's *Lord Hay's Masque*?" *Notes & Queries*, new series, 26 (1979): 144–45.

———, ed. *The Court Masque*. Manchester: Manchester University Press, 1984.

Lockyer, Roger. *Buckingham: The Life and Political Career of George Villiers, First Duke of Buckingham 1592–1628*. London and New York: Longman, 1981.

McGee, C. E. and John C. Meagher. "Preliminary Checklist of Tudor and Stuart Entertainments: 1614–1625." *Research Opportunities in Renaissance Drama* 30 (1988): 17–128.

McGowan, Margaret M. *L'Art du Ballet de Cour en France 1581–1643*. Paris: CNRS, 1963.

Mailliet, Marc de. *Ode a la lovange du serenissime Roy de la Grande Bretaigne*. London, 1617.

Malherbe, *Œuvres*. Ed. Antoine Adam. Paris: Gallimard, 1971.

Malone Society. "Dramatic Records in the Declared Accounts of the Treasurer of the Chamber 1588–1642." *Collections* 6 (1961 [1962]).

———. "Dramatic Records in the Declared Accounts of the Office of Works 1560–1640." *Collections* 10 (1975 [1977]).

———. "Jacobean and Caroline Revels Accounts, 1603–1642." *Collections* 13 (1986).

———. "Jacobean Academic Plays." *Collections* 14 (1988).

Marcus, Leah S. *The Politics of Mirth: Jonson, Herrick, Milton, Marvell, and the Defense of Old Holiday Pastimes*. Chicago and London: University of Chicago Press, 1986.

Meagher, John C. *Method and Meaning in Jonson's Masques*. Notre Dame, Ind. and London: University of Notre Dame Press, 1966.

Michaelis, Adolf. *Ancient Marbles in Great Britain*. Trans. C. A. M. Fennell. Cambridge, 1882.

Middleton, Thomas. *Honorable Entertainments*. Ed. R. C. Bald. Oxford: Malone Society, 1953.

———. *The Works of Thomas Middleton*. Ed. A. H. Bullen. 8 vols. London, 1885–86.

Nagler, A. M. *Theatre Festivals of the Medici, 1539–1637*. New Haven and London: Yale University Press, 1964.

Nevinson, John L. "A Show of the Nine Worthies." *Shakespeare Quarterly* 14 (1963): 103–07.

Nichols, John. *The Progresses, Processions, and Magnificent Entries of James the First*. 4 vols. London, 1828.

Nicoll, Allardyce. *Stuart Masques and the Renaissance Stage*. London: Harrap, 1938.

Orgel, Stephen. *The Illusion of Power: Political Theater in the English Renaissance.* Berkeley, Los Angeles, and London: University of California Press, 1975.

———. *The Jonsonian Masque.* Cambridge, Mass.: Harvard University Press, 1965.

——— and Roy Strong. *Inigo Jones: The Theatre of the Stuart Court.* 2 vols. Berkeley and Los Angeles: University of California Press; London: Sotheby Parke Bernet, 1973.

Orrell, John. "Buckingham's Patronage of the Dramatic Arts: The Crowe Accounts." *Records of the Early English Drama Newsletter* 2 (1980): 8–17.

———. "The London Court Stage in the Savoy Correspondence, 1613–1675." *Theatre Research International* 4 (1979): 79–94.

[Osborne, Francis]. *Historical Memoires on the Reign of Queen Elizabeth, and King James.* London, 1658.

Parkes, M. B. *Pause and Effect: An Introduction to the History of Punctuation in the West.* Berkeley and Los Angeles: University of California Press, 1993.

Parry, Graham. *The Golden Age Restor'd: The Culture of the Stuart Court, 1603–42.* Manchester: Manchester University Press, 1981.

Partridge, A. C. *Orthography in Shakespeare and Elizabethan Drama: A Study of Colloquial Contractions, Elision, Prosody and Punctuation.* Lincoln, Nebr.: University of Nebraska Press, 1964.

Peacock, John. "The French Element in Inigo Jones's Masque Designs." In David Lindley, ed., *The Court Masque*, 149–68. Manchester: Manchester University Press, 1984.

———. "Inigo Jones and the Arundel Marbles." *Journal of Medieval and Renaissance Studies* 16 (1986): 75–90.

———. *The Stage Designs of Inigo Jones: The European Context.* Cambridge: Cambridge University Press, 1995.

Pearl, Sara. "Sounding to present occasions: Jonson's masques of 1620–5." In David Lindley, ed., *The Court Masque*, 60–77. Manchester: Manchester University Press, 1984.

Peck, Linda Levy, ed. *The Mental World of the Jacobean Court.* Cambridge: Cambridge University Press, 1991.

Petti, Anthony G. *English Literary Hands from Chaucer to Dryden.* Cambridge, Mass.: Harvard University Press, 1977.

Portal, Ethel M. "The Academ Roial of King James I." *Proceedings of the British Academy* 7 (1915–16): 189–208.

Prunières, Henri. *Le Ballet de Cour en France avant Benserade et Lully.* 1914. Reprint, New York: Johnson Reprint, 1970.

Raggio, Olga. "The Myth of Prometheus: Its Survival and Metamorphoses up to the Eighteenth Century." *Journal of the Warburg and Courtauld Institutes* 21 (1958): 44–62.

Randall, Dale J. B. *Jonson's Gypsies Unmasked: Background and Theme of* The Gypsies Metamorphos'd. Durham, N. C.: Duke University Press, 1975.

Raylor, Timothy. "The Design and Authorship of *The Essex House Masque* (1621)." *Medieval & Renaissance Drama in England* 10 (1998): 218–37.

———. "The 'Lost' *Essex House Masque* (1621): A Manuscript Text Discovered." *English Manuscript Studies 1100–1700* 7 (1998), 86–130.

———. "Who Danced in *The Essex House Masque* (1621)?" *Notes & Queries*, new series 44 (1997): 530–33.

Raymond, Thomas. *Autobiography of Thomas Raymond.* Ed. G. Davies. Camden Society, 3d series, 28. London, 1917.

Reese, Jack E., "Unity in Chapman's *Masque of the Middle Temple and Lincoln's Inn.*" *Studies in English Literature* 4 (1964): 291–305.

Reyher, Paul. *Les Masques Anglais: Étude sur les Ballets et la vie de Cour en Angleterre (1512–1640).* Paris: Hachette, 1909.

Rousset, Jean. *La Littérature de l'Age Baroque en France: Circé et le Paon.* Paris: Corti, 1954.

Rubens, Peter Paul. *The Letters of Peter Paul Rubens.* Trans. and ed. Ruth Saunders Magurn. Cambridge, Mass.: Harvard University Press, 1955.

Russell, Conrad. *Parliaments and English Politics 1621–1629.* Oxford: Oxford University Press, 1979.

Sabbattini, Nicola. *Pratica di Fabricar Scene e Machine ne' Teatri* (1638). Trans. John H. McDowell. In Barnard Hewitt, ed., *The Renaissance Stage: Documents of Serlio, Sabbattini and Furttenbach*, 37–177. Coral Gables: University of Miami Press, 1958.

Sabol, Andrew J., ed. *Four Hundred Songs and Dances from the Stuart Masque.* Providence, R. I.: Brown University Press, 1978.

————, ed. *A Score for* The Lords' Masque *by Thomas Campion*. Hanover and London: University Press of New England, 1993.

————, ed. *A Score for* Lovers Made Men: *A Masque by Ben Jonson*. Providence, R. I.: Brown University Press, 1963.

Sandys, George. *Ovid's Metamorphosis Englished, Mythologiz'd, and Represented in Figures*. Ed. Karl K. Hulley and Stanley T. Vandersall. Lincoln, Nebr.: University of Nebraska Press, 1970.

Schoenbaum, S. *Internal Evidence and Elizabethan Dramatic Authorship: An Essay in Literary History and Method*. Evanston: Northwestern University Press, 1966.

Schreiber, Roy E. *The First Carlisle: Sir James Hay, First Earl of Carlisle as Courtier, Diplomat and Entrepeneur, 1580–1636*. Transactions of the American Philosophical Society. Vol. 74, number 7. Philadelphia, 1984.

————. *The Political Career of Sir Robert Naunton 1589–1635*. London: Royal Historical Society, 1981.

Schroeder, Horst. *Der Topos der Nine Worthies in Literatur und bildener Kunst*. Göttingen: Vandenhoeck and Ruprecht, 1971.

————. "The Mural Paintings of the Nine Worthies at Amersham." *Archaeological Journal* 138 (1981): 241–47.

Sellin, Paul R. "The Politics of Ben Jonson's *Newes from the New World Discover'd in the Moon*." *Viator* 17 (1986): 321–27.

————. *"So Doth, So Is Religion": John Donne and Diplomatic Contexts in the Reformed Netherlands, 1619–1620*. Columbia, Mo.: University of Missouri Press, 1988.

Shirley, John W. *Thomas Harriot: A Biography*. Oxford: Clarendon Press, 1983.

Sibley, Gertrude Marion. *The Lost Plays and Masques 1500–1642*. 1931. Reprint, New York: Russell & Russell, 1971.

Silvestris, Bernardus. *Commentary on the First Six Books of Virgil's Aeneid*. Trans. and ed. Earl G. Schreiber and Thomas E. Maresca. Lincoln, Nebr., and London: University of Nebraska Press, 1979.

Sisson, C. J. and Robert Butman. "George Chapman, 1612–22: Some New Facts." *Modern Language Review* 46 (1951): 185–90.

Sommerville, J. P. "James I and the divine right of kings: English politics and continental theory." In Peck, Linda Levy, ed., *The Mental World of the Jacobean Court*, 55–70. Cambridge: Cambridge University Press, 1991.

Spencer, T. J. B. and Stanley Wells, gen. eds. *A Book of Masques: In Honour of Allardyce Nicoll.* Cambridge: Cambridge University Press, 1967.

Stahlman, William D. and Owen Gingerich, *Solar and Planetary Longitudes for Years –2500 to +2000 by 10–Day Intervals.* Madison: University of Wisconsin Press, 1963.

Starnes, DeWitt T. and Ernest William Talbert. *Classical Myth and Legend in Renaissance Dictionaries: A Study of Renaissance Dictionaries in their Relation to the Classical Learning of Contemporary English Writers.* Chapel Hill: University of North Carolina Press, 1955.

Stead, Jennifer. "Bowers of Bliss: The Banquet Setting." In C. Anne Wilson, ed., *"Banquetting Stuffe": The Fare and Social Background of the Tudor and Stuart Banquet,* 115–57. Edinburgh: Edinburgh University Press, 1991.

Steele, Mary Susan. *Plays & Masques at Court during the Reigns of Elizabeth, James and Charles.* New Haven and London: Yale University Press, 1926.

Stone, Lawrence. *The Crisis of the Aristocracy 1558–1641.* Oxford: Clarendon Press, 1965.

Stuart Royal Proclamations. 1: *Royal Proclamations of King James I: 1603–1625.* Ed. James F. Larkin and Paul L. Hughes. Oxford: Clarendon Press, 1973.

Sylvester, Joshua. *The Second Session of Parliament of Vertues Real.* London, 1615.

Thorndike, Lynn. *A History of Magic and Experimental Science.* Vols. 5–6: *The Sixteenth Century.* New York: Columbia University Press, 1941.

Tillières, Comte Leveneur de. *Mémoires Inédits du Comte Leveneur de Tillières.* Ed. C. Hippeau. Paris, 1863.

Topsell, Edward. *A Historie of Foure-footed Beastes.* London, 1607.

Townshend, Aurelian. *The Poems and Masques of Aurelian Townshend.* Ed. Cedric C. Brown. Reading: Whiteknights Press, 1983.

Treip, Mindele. *Milton's Punctuation and Changing English Usage 1582–1676.* London: Methuen, 1970.

Trousson, Raymond. *Le Thème de Prométheé dans la Littérature Européenne.* 2 vols. Geneva: Droz, 1964.

Turnbull, G. H. "Samuel Hartlib's Connection with Sir Francis Kynaston's 'Musaeum Minervae.'" *Notes & Queries* 197 (1952): 33–37.

Verheyen, Egon. *The Palazzo del Te in Mantua: Images of Love and Politics*. Baltimore and London: Johns Hopkins University Press, 1977.

Viau, Théophile de. *Œuvres Poétiques*. Ed. Guido Saba. Paris: Garnier, 1990.

Waddington, Raymond B. *The Mind's Empire: Myth and Form in George Chapman's Narrative Poems*. Baltimore and London: Johns Hopkins University Press, 1974.

Walker, D. P. *Spiritual and Demonic Magic from Ficino to Campanella*. London: Warburg Institute, 1958.

Walls, Peter. "Insubstantial Pageants Preserved: the Literary and Musical Sources for the Jonsonian Masque." In Ian Donaldson, ed., *Jonson and Shakespeare*, 202–18. Atlantic Highlands, N. J.: Humanities Press, 1983.

———. "The Origins of English Recitative." *Proceedings of the Royal Musical Association* 110 (1983–84): 25–40.

Weckherlin, George Rudolf. *A Panegyricke To the most honourable and renowned Lord, The Lord Hays*. Stuttgart, 1619.

Weldon, Anthony. *The Court and Character of King James*. London, 1650.

Welsford, Enid. *The Court Masque: A Study in the Relationship between Poetry & the Revels*. Cambridge: Cambridge University Press, 1927.

White, Christopher. *Anthony Van Dyck: Thomas Howard The Earl of Arundel*. Malibu, Calif.: Getty Museum, 1995.

Wickham, Glynne. *Early English Stages 1300–1600. Volume 1: 1300–1576*. 2d ed. London and Henley: RKP; New York: Columbia University Press, 1980.

———. *Early English Stages 1300–1660. Volume Two: 1576–1660, Part 1*. London: RKP, 1963.

———. *Early English Stages 1300–1660. Volume Two: 1576–1660, Part 2*. London: RKP, 1972.

Wilson, Arthur. *The History of Great Britain: being the life and reign of King James the First*. London, 1653.

———. *The Narrative History of King James, for the first fourteen Years*. London, 1651.

Wilson, C. Anne. "The Evolution of the Banquet Course: Some Medicinal, Culinary and Social Aspects." In C. Anne Wilson, ed.,

"Banquetting Stuffe": The Fare and Social Background of the *Tudor and Stuart Banquet*, 9–35. Edinburgh: Edinburgh University Press, 1991.

————. *Food & Drink in Britain from the Stone Age to recent times.* London: Constable, 1973.

————, ed. *"Banquetting Stuffe": The Fare and Social Background of the Tudor and Stuart Banquet.* Edinburgh: Edinburgh University Press, 1991.

Wind, Edgar. *Pagan Mysteries in the Renaissance.* Rev. ed. New York and London: Norton, 1968.

Yates, Frances A. *Astraea: The Imperial Theme in the Sixteenth Century.* London and New York: RKP, 1975.

————. *The French Academies of the Sixteenth Century.* London: Warburg Institute, 1947.

————. *Theatre of the World.* London and New York: RKP, 1969.

Yonge, Walter. *The Diary of Walter Yonge.* Ed. George Roberts, Camden Society 41. London, 1848.

Young, Alan R. *The English Tournament Imprese.* New York: AMS, 1988.

Zaller, Robert. *The Parliament of 1621: A Study in Constitutional Conflict.* Berkeley, Los Angeles, and London: University of California Press, 1971.

INDEX